Muffins & Breads

D0342122

Recipes to make your own gifts

Use these recipes to delight your friends and family. Each recipe includes gift tags for your convenience — just cut them out and personalize!

To decorate jars, cut fabric in 9" diameter circles. Screw down the jar ring to hold fabric in place or hold fabric with a ribbon, raffia, twine, yarn, lace, or string (first secure the fabric with a rubber band before tying). Punch a hole into the corner of the tag and use the ribbon, raffia, twine, yarn, lace, or string to attach the tag to the jar.

These gifts should keep for up to six months. If the mix contains nuts, it should be used within three months.

Printed in the United States of America
by G&R Publishing Co.

Second Edition

Distributed By:

507 Industrial Street
Waverly, IA 50677

ISBN 1-56383-122-8
Item #3002

Ginger Spice Muffin Mix

3 1/2 C. all-purpose flour
1/4 C. sugar
1 T. baking powder
1 tsp. baking soda
2 tsp. ground cinnamon
1 tsp. ground nutmeg
1/2 tsp. ground ginger
1/2 tsp. ground cloves
1 tsp. salt

Layer the ingredients in the order given into a wide-mouth 1-quart canning jar. Pack each layer in place before adding the next ingredient.

Attach a gift tag with the mixing and baking directions.

Ginger Spice Muffins

1 jar Ginger Spice Muffin Mix
1/2 C. butter or margarine,
  melted
2 eggs, slightly beaten
2 tsp. vanilla
2 C. milk

Preheat the oven to 400°F. In a large bowl, combine the Ginger Spice Muffin Mix with the butter, eggs, vanilla and milk. Stir until the mixture is just blended. Do not overmix. Spoon the batter into greased muffin tins, filling 2/3 to 3/4 full. Bake for 15 to 18 minutes, or until golden brown. Serve warm or cool completely on a wire rack.

Ginger Spice Muffins

1 jar Ginger Spice Muffin Mix	2 eggs, slightly beaten
1/2 C. butter or margarine, melted	2 tsp. vanilla
	2 C. milk

Preheat the oven to 400°F. In a large bowl, combine the Ginger Spice Muffin Mix with the butter, eggs, vanilla and milk. Stir until the mixture is just blended. Do not overmix. Spoon the batter into greased muffin tins, filling 2/3 to 3/4 full. Bake for 15 to 18 minutes, or until golden brown. Serve warm or cool completely on a wire rack.

Ginger Spice Muffins

1 jar Ginger Spice Muffin Mix	2 eggs, slightly beaten
1/2 C. butter or margarine, melted	2 tsp. vanilla
	2 C. milk

Preheat the oven to 400°F. In a large bowl, combine the Ginger Spice Muffin Mix with the butter, eggs, vanilla and milk. Stir until the mixture is just blended. Do not overmix. Spoon the batter into greased muffin tins, filling 2/3 to 3/4 full. Bake for 15 to 18 minutes, or until golden brown. Serve warm or cool completely on a wire rack.

Ginger Spice Muffins

1 jar Ginger Spice Muffin Mix	2 eggs, slightly beaten
1/2 C. butter or margarine, melted	2 tsp. vanilla
	2 C. milk

Preheat the oven to 400°F. In a large bowl, combine the Ginger Spice Muffin Mix with the butter, eggs, vanilla and milk. Stir until the mixture is just blended. Do not overmix. Spoon the batter into greased muffin tins, filling 2/3 to 3/4 full. Bake for 15 to 18 minutes, or until golden brown. Serve warm or cool completely on a wire rack.

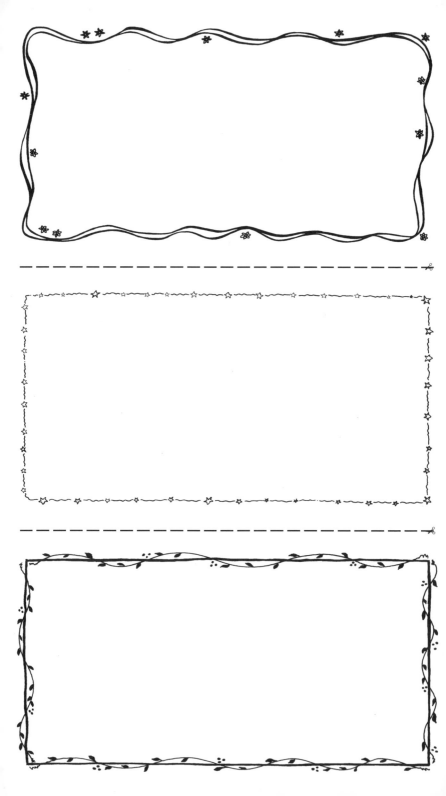

Ginger Spice Muffins

1 jar Ginger Spice Muffin Mix	2 eggs, slightly beaten
1/2 C. butter or margarine, melted	2 tsp. vanilla
	2 C. milk

Preheat the oven to 400°F. In a large bowl, combine the Ginger Spice Muffin Mix with the butter, eggs, vanilla and milk. Stir until the mixture is just blended. Do not overmix. Spoon the batter into greased muffin tins, filling 2/3 to 3/4 full. Bake for 15 to 18 minutes, or until golden brown. Serve warm or cool completely on a wire rack.

Ginger Spice Muffins

1 jar Ginger Spice Muffin Mix	2 eggs, slightly beaten
1/2 C. butter or margarine, melted	2 tsp. vanilla
	2 C. milk

Preheat the oven to 400°F. In a large bowl, combine the Ginger Spice Muffin Mix with the butter, eggs, vanilla and milk. Stir until the mixture is just blended. Do not overmix. Spoon the batter into greased muffin tins, filling 2/3 to 3/4 full. Bake for 15 to 18 minutes, or until golden brown. Serve warm or cool completely on a wire rack.

Ginger Spice Muffins

1 jar Ginger Spice Muffin Mix	2 eggs, slightly beaten
1/2 C. butter or margarine, melted	2 tsp. vanilla
	2 C. milk

Preheat the oven to 400°F. In a large bowl, combine the Ginger Spice Muffin Mix with the butter, eggs, vanilla and milk. Stir until the mixture is just blended. Do not overmix. Spoon the batter into greased muffin tins, filling 2/3 to 3/4 full. Bake for 15 to 18 minutes, or until golden brown. Serve warm or cool completely on a wire rack.

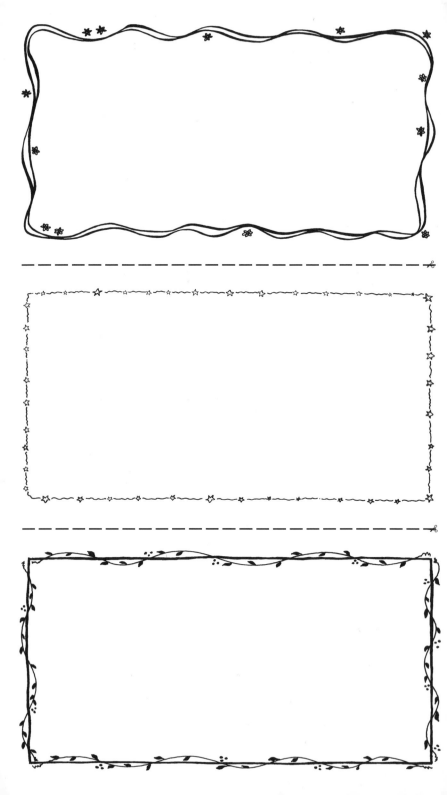

Apple Muffin Mix

1/2 C. sugar
1 1/2 tsp. baking powder
1/4 C. brown sugar
1 tsp. cinnamon
1/4 tsp. nutmeg
1 C. chopped dried apple
2 C. flour

Layer the ingredients in the order given into a wide-mouth 1-quart canning jar. Pack each layer in place before adding the next ingredient.

Attach a gift tag with the mixing and baking directions.

Apple Muffins

1 jar Apple Muffin Mix
1 egg, slightly beaten
3/4 C. milk
1/4 C. oil

Preheat the oven to 400°F. In a large bowl, combine the Apple Muffin Mix with the egg, milk and oil. Stir until the mixture is just blended. Do not overmix. Spoon the batter into greased muffin tins, filling 2/3 to 3/4 full. Bake for 15 to 18 minutes, or until golden brown. Serve warm or cool completely on a wire rack.

Apple Muffins

1 jar Apple Muffin Mix   3/4 C. milk
1 egg, slightly beaten   1/4 C. oil

Preheat the oven to 400°F. In a large bowl, combine the Apple Muffin Mix with the egg, milk and oil. Stir until the mixture is just blended. Do not overmix. Spoon the batter into greased muffin tins, filling 2/3 to 3/4 full. Bake for 15 to 18 minutes, or until golden brown. Serve warm or cool completely on a wire rack.

Apple Muffins

1 jar Apple Muffin Mix   3/4 C. milk
1 egg, slightly beaten   1/4 C. oil

Preheat the oven to 400°F. In a large bowl, combine the Apple Muffin Mix with the egg, milk and oil. Stir until the mixture is just blended. Do not overmix. Spoon the batter into greased muffin tins, filling 2/3 to 3/4 full. Bake for 15 to 18 minutes, or until golden brown. Serve warm or cool completely on a wire rack.

Apple Muffins

1 jar Apple Muffin Mix   3/4 C. milk
1 egg, slightly beaten   1/4 C. oil

Preheat the oven to 400°F. In a large bowl, combine the Apple Muffin Mix with the egg, milk and oil. Stir until the mixture is just blended. Do not overmix. Spoon the batter into greased muffin tins, filling 2/3 to 3/4 full. Bake for 15 to 18 minutes, or until golden brown. Serve warm or cool completely on a wire rack.

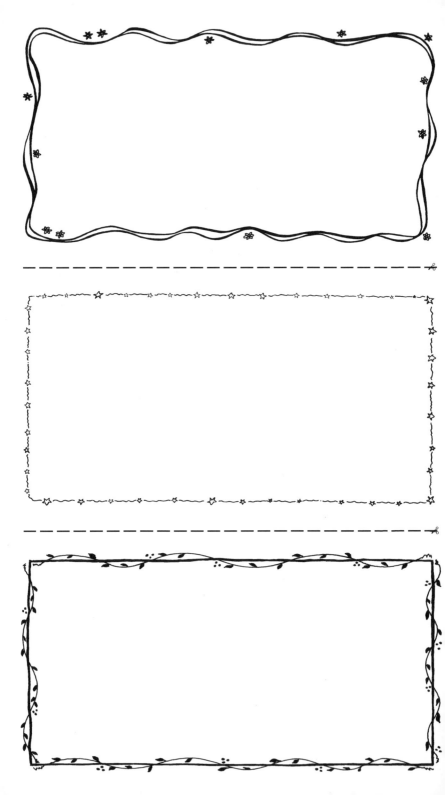

Apple Muffins

1 jar Apple Muffin Mix   3/4 C. milk
1 egg, slightly beaten   1/4 C. oil

Preheat the oven to 400°F. In a large bowl, combine the Apple Muffin Mix with the egg, milk and oil. Stir until the mixture is just blended. Do not overmix. Spoon the batter into greased muffin tins, filling 2/3 to 3/4 full. Bake for 15 to 18 minutes, or until golden brown. Serve warm or cool completely on a wire rack.

Apple Muffins

1 jar Apple Muffin Mix   3/4 C. milk
1 egg, slightly beaten   1/4 C. oil

Preheat the oven to 400°F. In a large bowl, combine the Apple Muffin Mix with the egg, milk and oil. Stir until the mixture is just blended. Do not overmix. Spoon the batter into greased muffin tins, filling 2/3 to 3/4 full. Bake for 15 to 18 minutes, or until golden brown. Serve warm or cool completely on a wire rack.

Apple Muffins

1 jar Apple Muffin Mix   3/4 C. milk
1 egg, slightly beaten   1/4 C. oil

Preheat the oven to 400°F. In a large bowl, combine the Apple Muffin Mix with the egg, milk and oil. Stir until the mixture is just blended. Do not overmix. Spoon the batter into greased muffin tins, filling 2/3 to 3/4 full. Bake for 15 to 18 minutes, or until golden brown. Serve warm or cool completely on a wire rack.

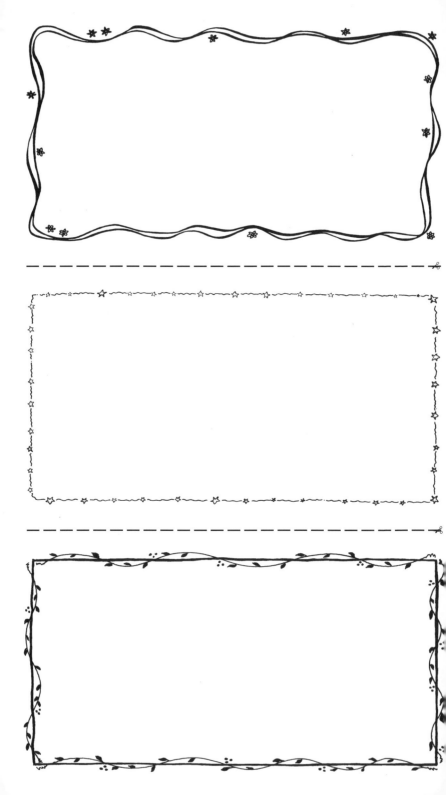

Date & Nut Muffin Mix

2 C. self-rising flour
1/2 C. sugar
1/4 C. brown sugar
1 tsp. cinnamon
1/4 tsp. nutmeg
1 C. chopped pecans

Layer the ingredients in the order given into a wide-mouth 1-quart canning jar. Pack each layer in place before adding the next ingredient.

Attach a gift tag with the mixing and baking directions.

❀ A half-yard of fabric should make eight wide-mouth jar covers. ❀

Date & Nut Muffins

1 jar Date & Nut Muffin Mix
1 egg, slightly beaten
3/4 C. milk
2/3 C. chopped dates
1/4 C. oil

Preheat the oven to 400°F. In a large bowl, combine the Date & Nut Muffin Mix with the egg, milk, dates and oil. Stir until the mixture is just blended. Do not overmix. Spoon the batter into greased muffin tins, filling 2/3 to 3/4 full. Bake for 15 to 18 minutes, or until golden brown. Serve warm or cool completely on a wire rack.

Date & Nut Muffins

1 jar Date & Nut Muffin Mix
1 egg, slightly beaten
3/4 C. milk

2/3 C. chopped dates
1/4 C. oil

Preheat the oven to 400°F. In a large bowl, combine the Date & Nut Muffin Mix with the egg, milk, dates and oil. Stir until the mixture is just blended. Do not overmix. Spoon the batter into greased muffin tins, filling 2/3 to 3/4 full. Bake for 15 to 18 minutes, or until golden brown. Serve warm or cool completely on a wire rack.

Date & Nut Muffins

1 jar Date & Nut Muffin Mix
1 egg, slightly beaten
3/4 C. milk

2/3 C. chopped dates
1/4 C. oil

Preheat the oven to 400°F. In a large bowl, combine the Date & Nut Muffin Mix with the egg, milk, dates and oil. Stir until the mixture is just blended. Do not overmix. Spoon the batter into greased muffin tins, filling 2/3 to 3/4 full. Bake for 15 to 18 minutes, or until golden brown. Serve warm or cool completely on a wire rack.

Date & Nut Muffins

1 jar Date & Nut Muffin Mix
1 egg, slightly beaten
3/4 C. milk

2/3 C. chopped dates
1/4 C. oil

Preheat the oven to 400°F. In a large bowl, combine the Date & Nut Muffin Mix with the egg, milk, dates and oil. Stir until the mixture is just blended. Do not overmix. Spoon the batter into greased muffin tins, filling 2/3 to 3/4 full. Bake for 15 to 18 minutes, or until golden brown. Serve warm or cool completely on a wire rack.

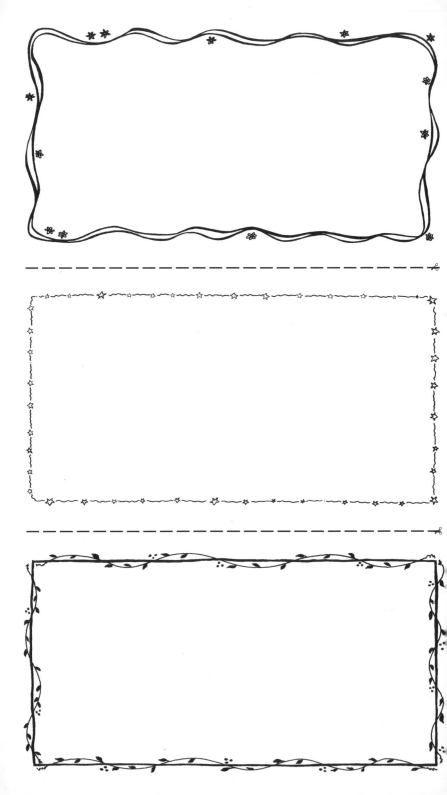

Date & Nut Muffins

1 jar Date & Nut Muffin Mix
1 egg, slightly beaten
3/4 C. milk

2/3 C. chopped dates
1/4 C. oil

Preheat the oven to 400°F. In a large bowl, combine the Date & Nut Muffin Mix with the egg, milk, dates and oil. Stir until the mixture is just blended. Do not overmix. Spoon the batter into greased muffin tins, filling 2/3 to 3/4 full. Bake for 15 to 18 minutes, or until golden brown. Serve warm or cool completely on a wire rack.

Date & Nut Muffins

1 jar Date & Nut Muffin Mix
1 egg, slightly beaten
3/4 C. milk

2/3 C. chopped dates
1/4 C. oil

Preheat the oven to 400°F. In a large bowl, combine the Date & Nut Muffin Mix with the egg, milk, dates and oil. Stir until the mixture is just blended. Do not overmix. Spoon the batter into greased muffin tins, filling 2/3 to 3/4 full. Bake for 15 to 18 minutes, or until golden brown. Serve warm or cool completely on a wire rack.

Date & Nut Muffins

1 jar Date & Nut Muffin Mix
1 egg, slightly beaten
3/4 C. milk

2/3 C. chopped dates
1/4 C. oil

Preheat the oven to 400°F. In a large bowl, combine the Date & Nut Muffin Mix with the egg, milk, dates and oil. Stir until the mixture is just blended. Do not overmix. Spoon the batter into greased muffin tins, filling 2/3 to 3/4 full. Bake for 15 to 18 minutes, or until golden brown. Serve warm or cool completely on a wire rack.

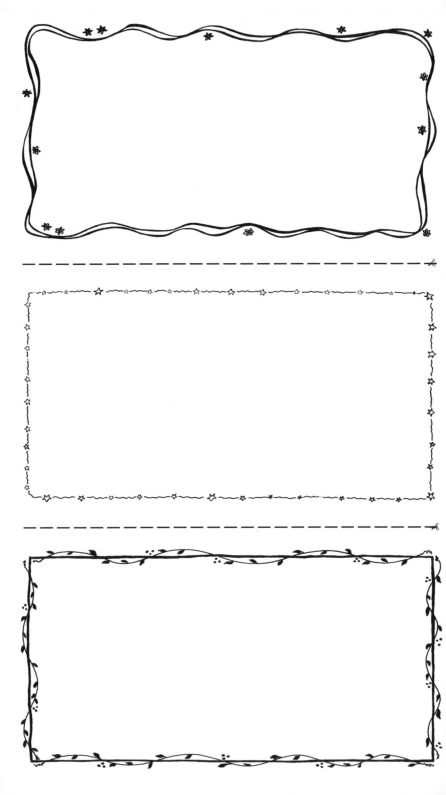

Bran Muffin Mix

2 C. All-Bran cereal
1 1/4 C. self-rising flour
1/2 C. sugar
1/2 C. golden raisins
1 T. baking powder
1/4 tsp. salt

Layer the ingredients in the order given into a wide-mouth 1-quart canning jar. Pack each layer in place before adding the next ingredient.

Attach a gift tag with the mixing and baking directions.

Bran Muffins

1 jar Bran Muffin Mix
1/4 C. vegetable oil
1 1/4 C. milk
1 egg, slightly beaten

Preheat the oven to 400°F. In a large bowl, combine the Bran Muffin Mix with the butter, milk and egg. Stir until the mixture is just blended. Do not overmix. Spoon the batter into greased muffin tins, filling 2/3 to 3/4 full. Bake for 16 to 18 minutes, or until golden brown. Serve warm or cool completely on a wire rack.

Pineapple Bran Muffins

Add one 8-ounce can crushed pineapple, which has been drained, to the batter.

Bran Muffins

1 jar Bran Muffin Mix   1 1/4 C. milk
1/4 C. vegetable oil   1 egg, slightly beaten

Preheat the oven to 400°F. In a large bowl, combine the Bran Muffin Mix with the butter, milk and egg. Stir until the mixture is just blended. Do not overmix. Spoon the batter into greased muffin tins, filling 2/3 to 3/4 full. Bake for 16 to 18 minutes, or until golden brown. Serve warm or cool completely on a wire rack.

Pineapple Bran Muffins

Add one 8-ounce can crushed pineapple, which has been drained, to the batter.

Bran Muffins

1 jar Bran Muffin Mix   1 1/4 C. milk
1/4 C. vegetable oil   1 egg, slightly beaten

Preheat the oven to 400°F. In a large bowl, combine the Bran Muffin Mix with the butter, milk and egg. Stir until the mixture is just blended. Do not overmix. Spoon the batter into greased muffin tins, filling 2/3 to 3/4 full. Bake for 16 to 18 minutes, or until golden brown. Serve warm or cool completely on a wire rack.

Pineapple Bran Muffins

Add one 8-ounce can crushed pineapple, which has been drained, to the batter.

Bran Muffins

1 jar Bran Muffin Mix   1 1/4 C. milk
1/4 C. vegetable oil   1 egg, slightly beaten

Preheat the oven to 400°F. In a large bowl, combine the Bran Muffin Mix with the butter, milk and egg. Stir until the mixture is just blended. Do not overmix. Spoon the batter into greased muffin tins, filling 2/3 to 3/4 full. Bake for 16 to 18 minutes, or until golden brown. Serve warm or cool completely on a wire rack.

Pineapple Bran Muffins

Add one 8-ounce can crushed pineapple, which has been drained, to the batter.

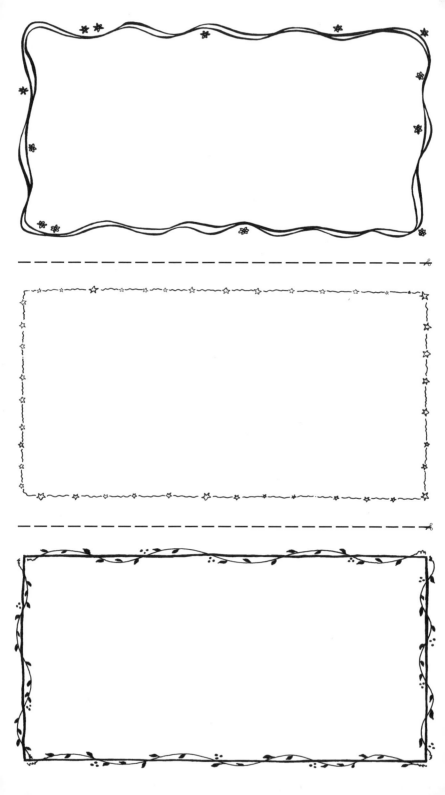

Bran Muffins

1 jar Bran Muffin Mix   1 1/4 C. milk
1/4 C. vegetable oil   1 egg, slightly beaten

Preheat the oven to 400°F. In a large bowl, combine the Bran Muffin Mix with the butter, milk and egg. Stir until the mixture is just blended. Do not overmix. Spoon the batter into greased muffin tins, filling 2/3 to 3/4 full. Bake for 16 to 18 minutes, or until golden brown. Serve warm or cool completely on a wire rack.

Pineapple Bran Muffins

Add one 8-ounce can crushed pineapple, which has been drained, to the batter.

Bran Muffins

1 jar Bran Muffin Mix   1 1/4 C. milk
1/4 C. vegetable oil   1 egg, slightly beaten

Preheat the oven to 400°F. In a large bowl, combine the Bran Muffin Mix with the butter, milk and egg. Stir until the mixture is just blended. Do not overmix. Spoon the batter into greased muffin tins, filling 2/3 to 3/4 full. Bake for 16 to 18 minutes, or until golden brown. Serve warm or cool completely on a wire rack.

Pineapple Bran Muffins

Add one 8-ounce can crushed pineapple, which has been drained, to the batter.

Bran Muffins

1 jar Bran Muffin Mix   1 1/4 C. milk
1/4 C. vegetable oil   1 egg, slightly beaten

Preheat the oven to 400°F. In a large bowl, combine the Bran Muffin Mix with the butter, milk and egg. Stir until the mixture is just blended. Do not overmix. Spoon the batter into greased muffin tins, filling 2/3 to 3/4 full. Bake for 16 to 18 minutes, or until golden brown. Serve warm or cool completely on a wire rack.

Pineapple Bran Muffins

Add one 8-ounce can crushed pineapple, which has been drained, to the batter.

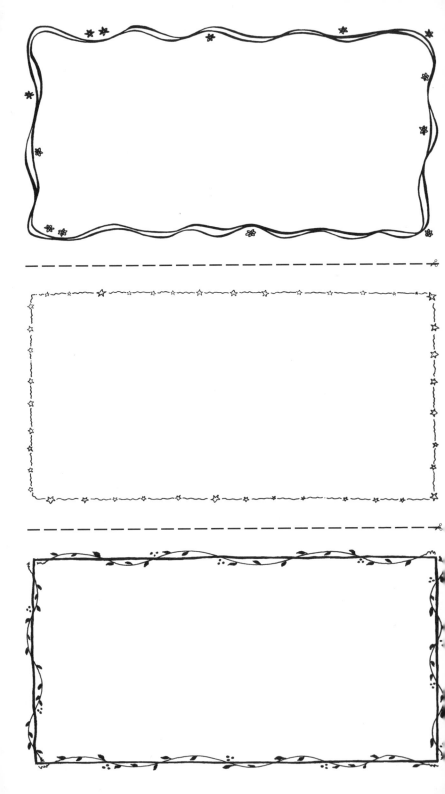

Chocolate Chip Muffin Mix

2 C. all-purpose flour
1 1/2 tsp. baking powder
1/2 tsp. baking soda
1 tsp. ground cinnamon
1/2 tsp. ground nutmeg
1/8 tsp. salt
2/3 C. brown sugar
1/2 C. chocolate chips

Layer the ingredients in the order given into a wide-mouth 1-quart canning jar. Pack each layer in place before adding the next ingredient.

Attach a gift tag with the mixing and baking directions.

Chocolate Chip Muffins

1 jar Chocolate Chip Muffin Mix
3/4 C. buttermilk
3/4 C. applesauce
1 egg, slightly beaten
1 1/2 T. vegetable oil
1 tsp. vanilla

Preheat the oven to 350°F. In a large bowl, combine the Chocolate Chip Muffin Mix with the buttermilk, applesauce, egg, oil and vanilla. Stir until the mixture is just blended. Do not overmix. Spoon the batter into greased muffin tins, filling 2/3 to 3/4 full. Bake for 18 to 20 minutes, or until golden brown. Cool on a wire rack for 10 minutes before removing. Serve warm or cool completely on a wire rack.

Chocolate Chip Muffins

1 jar Chocolate Chip Muffin Mix	1 egg, slightly beaten
3/4 C. buttermilk	1 1/2 T. vegetable oil
3/4 C. applesauce	1 tsp. vanilla

Preheat the oven to 350°F. In a large bowl, combine the Chocolate Chip Muffin Mix with the buttermilk, applesauce, egg, oil and vanilla. Stir until the mixture is just blended. Do not overmix. Spoon the batter into greased muffin tins, filling 2/3 to 3/4 full. Bake for 18 to 20 minutes, or until golden brown. Cool on a wire rack for 10 minutes before removing. Serve warm or cool completely on a wire rack.

Chocolate Chip Muffins

1 jar Chocolate Chip Muffin Mix	1 egg, slightly beaten
3/4 C. buttermilk	1 1/2 T. vegetable oil
3/4 C. applesauce	1 tsp. vanilla

Preheat the oven to 350°F. In a large bowl, combine the Chocolate Chip Muffin Mix with the buttermilk, applesauce, egg, oil and vanilla. Stir until the mixture is just blended. Do not overmix. Spoon the batter into greased muffin tins, filling 2/3 to 3/4 full. Bake for 18 to 20 minutes, or until golden brown. Cool on a wire rack for 10 minutes before removing. Serve warm or cool completely on a wire rack.

Chocolate Chip Muffins

1 jar Chocolate Chip Muffin Mix	1 egg, slightly beaten
3/4 C. buttermilk	1 1/2 T. vegetable oil
3/4 C. applesauce	1 tsp. vanilla

Preheat the oven to 350°F. In a large bowl, combine the Chocolate Chip Muffin Mix with the buttermilk, applesauce, egg, oil and vanilla. Stir until the mixture is just blended. Do not overmix. Spoon the batter into greased muffin tins, filling 2/3 to 3/4 full. Bake for 18 to 20 minutes, or until golden brown. Cool on a wire rack for 10 minutes before removing. Serve warm or cool completely on a wire rack.

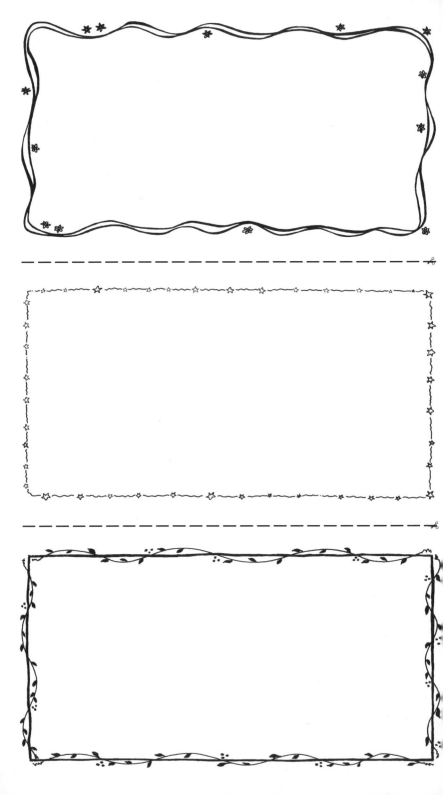

Chocolate Chip Muffins

1 jar Chocolate Chip Muffin Mix
3/4 C. buttermilk
3/4 C. applesauce

1 egg, slightly beaten
1 1/2 T. vegetable oil
1 tsp. vanilla

Preheat the oven to 350°F. In a large bowl, combine the Chocolate Chip Muffin Mix with the buttermilk, applesauce, egg, oil and vanilla. Stir until the mixture is just blended. Do not overmix. Spoon the batter into greased muffin tins, filling 2/3 to 3/4 full. Bake for 18 to 20 minutes, or until golden brown. Cool on a wire rack for 10 minutes before removing. Serve warm or cool completely on a wire rack.

Chocolate Chip Muffins

1 jar Chocolate Chip Muffin Mix
3/4 C. buttermilk
3/4 C. applesauce

1 egg, slightly beaten
1 1/2 T. vegetable oil
1 tsp. vanilla

Preheat the oven to 350°F. In a large bowl, combine the Chocolate Chip Muffin Mix with the buttermilk, applesauce, egg, oil and vanilla. Stir until the mixture is just blended. Do not overmix. Spoon the batter into greased muffin tins, filling 2/3 to 3/4 full. Bake for 18 to 20 minutes, or until golden brown. Cool on a wire rack for 10 minutes before removing. Serve warm or cool completely on a wire rack.

Chocolate Chip Muffins

1 jar Chocolate Chip Muffin Mix
3/4 C. buttermilk
3/4 C. applesauce

1 egg, slightly beaten
1 1/2 T. vegetable oil
1 tsp. vanilla

Preheat the oven to 350°F. In a large bowl, combine the Chocolate Chip Muffin Mix with the buttermilk, applesauce, egg, oil and vanilla. Stir until the mixture is just blended. Do not overmix. Spoon the batter into greased muffin tins, filling 2/3 to 3/4 full. Bake for 18 to 20 minutes, or until golden brown. Cool on a wire rack for 10 minutes before removing. Serve warm or cool completely on a wire rack.

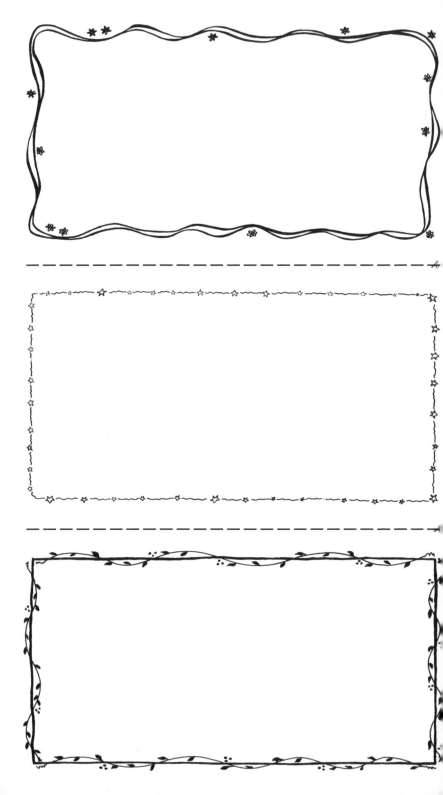

Heart Smart
Muffin Mix

2 C. all-purpose flour
1 1/2 tsp. baking powder
1/2 tsp. baking soda
1 tsp. ground cinnamon
1/2 tsp. ground nutmeg
1/8 tsp. salt
2/3 C. brown sugar
1/2 C. raisins, currants or
    walnuts

Layer the ingredients in the order given into a wide-mouth 1-quart canning jar. Pack each layer in place before adding the next ingredient.

Attach a gift tag with the mixing and baking directions.

Heart Smart Muffins

1 jar Heart Smart Muffin Mix
3/4 C. buttermilk
3/4 C. applesauce
1 egg, slightly beaten
1 1/2 T. vegetable oil
1 tsp. vanilla
1/2 C. fresh or frozen blueberries
   or raspberries if desired

Preheat the oven to 350°F. In a large bowl, combine the Heart Smart Muffin Mix with the buttermilk, applesauce, egg, oil and vanilla. Stir until the mixture is just blended. Do not overmix. Spoon the batter into greased muffin tins, filling 2/3 to 3/4 full. Bake for 18 to 20 minutes, or until golden brown. Cool on a wire rack for 10 minutes before removing. Serve warm or cool completely on a wire rack.

Heart Smart Muffins

1 jar Heart Smart Muffin Mix
3/4 C. buttermilk
3/4 C. applesauce
1 egg, slightly beaten
1 1/2 T. vegetable oil

1 tsp. vanilla
1/2 C. fresh or frozen
   blueberries or raspberries
   if desired

Preheat the oven to 350°F. In a large bowl, combine the Heart Smart Muffin Mix with the buttermilk, applesauce, egg, oil and vanilla. Stir until the mixture is just blended. Do not overmix. Spoon the batter into greased muffin tins, filling 2/3 to 3/4 full. Bake for 18 to 20 minutes, or until golden brown. Cool on a wire rack for 10 minutes before removing. Serve warm or cool completely on a wire rack.

Heart Smart Muffins

1 jar Heart Smart Muffin Mix
3/4 C. buttermilk
3/4 C. applesauce
1 egg, slightly beaten
1 1/2 T. vegetable oil

1 tsp. vanilla
1/2 C. fresh or frozen
   blueberries or raspberries
   if desired

Preheat the oven to 350°F. In a large bowl, combine the Heart Smart Muffin Mix with the buttermilk, applesauce, egg, oil and vanilla. Stir until the mixture is just blended. Do not overmix. Spoon the batter into greased muffin tins, filling 2/3 to 3/4 full. Bake for 18 to 20 minutes, or until golden brown. Cool on a wire rack for 10 minutes before removing. Serve warm or cool completely on a wire rack.

Heart Smart Muffins

1 jar Heart Smart Muffin Mix
3/4 C. buttermilk
3/4 C. applesauce
1 egg, slightly beaten
1 1/2 T. vegetable oil

1 tsp. vanilla
1/2 C. fresh or frozen
   blueberries or raspberries
   if desired

Preheat the oven to 350°F. In a large bowl, combine the Heart Smart Muffin Mix with the buttermilk, applesauce, egg, oil and vanilla. Stir until the mixture is just blended. Do not overmix. Spoon the batter into greased muffin tins, filling 2/3 to 3/4 full. Bake for 18 to 20 minutes, or until golden brown. Cool on a wire rack for 10 minutes before removing. Serve warm or cool completely on a wire rack.

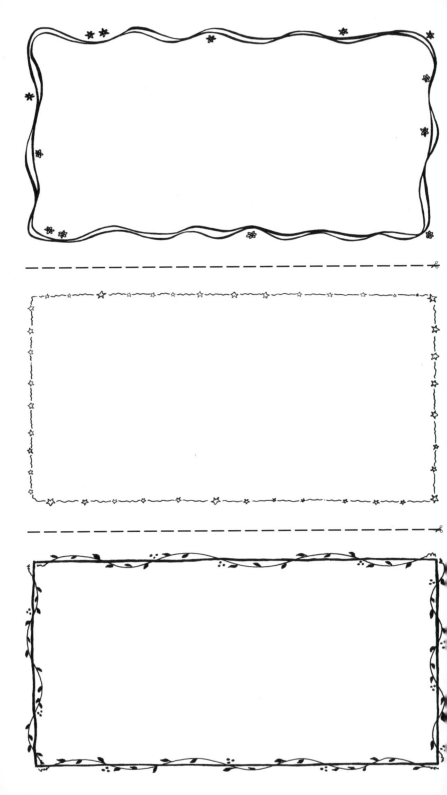

Heart Smart Muffins

1 jar Heart Smart Muffin Mix
3/4 C. buttermilk
3/4 C. applesauce
1 egg, slightly beaten
1 1/2 T. vegetable oil

1 tsp. vanilla
1/2 C. fresh or frozen
   blueberries or raspberries
   if desired

Preheat the oven to 350°F. In a large bowl, combine the Heart Smart Muffin Mix with the buttermilk, applesauce, egg, oil and vanilla. Stir until the mixture is just blended. Do not overmix. Spoon the batter into greased muffin tins, filling 2/3 to 3/4 full. Bake for 18 to 20 minutes, or until golden brown. Cool on a wire rack for 10 minutes before removing. Serve warm or cool completely on a wire rack.

Heart Smart Muffins

1 jar Heart Smart Muffin Mix
3/4 C. buttermilk
3/4 C. applesauce
1 egg, slightly beaten
1 1/2 T. vegetable oil

1 tsp. vanilla
1/2 C. fresh or frozen
   blueberries or raspberries
   if desired

Preheat the oven to 350°F. In a large bowl, combine the Heart Smart Muffin Mix with the buttermilk, applesauce, egg, oil and vanilla. Stir until the mixture is just blended. Do not overmix. Spoon the batter into greased muffin tins, filling 2/3 to 3/4 full. Bake for 18 to 20 minutes, or until golden brown. Cool on a wire rack for 10 minutes before removing. Serve warm or cool completely on a wire rack.

Heart Smart Muffins

1 jar Heart Smart Muffin Mix
3/4 C. buttermilk
3/4 C. applesauce
1 egg, slightly beaten
1 1/2 T. vegetable oil

1 tsp. vanilla
1/2 C. fresh or frozen
   blueberries or raspberries
   if desired

Preheat the oven to 350°F. In a large bowl, combine the Heart Smart Muffin Mix with the buttermilk, applesauce, egg, oil and vanilla. Stir until the mixture is just blended. Do not overmix. Spoon the batter into greased muffin tins, filling 2/3 to 3/4 full. Bake for 18 to 20 minutes, or until golden brown. Cool on a wire rack for 10 minutes before removing. Serve warm or cool completely on a wire rack.

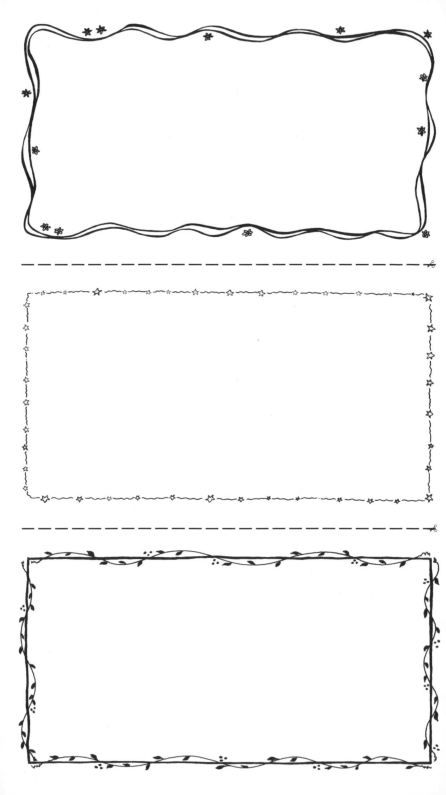

Holiday Muffin Mix

2 1/2 C. all-purpose flour
1/2 C. whole wheat flour
3/4 C. sugar
1/2 C. instant nonfat dry milk
2 T. baking powder
1 tsp. salt
1 T. cinnamon
1/2 tsp. ground cloves

Layer the ingredients in the order given into a wide-mouth 1-quart canning jar. Pack each layer in place before adding the next ingredient.

Attach a gift tag with the mixing and baking directions.

❀ For an out of the ordinary gift, try placing the mix in a mixing bowl along with kitchen utensils, cookbooks, recipe cards, towels, and pot holders. ❀

Holiday Muffins

1 jar Holiday Muffin Mix
1 1/3 C . water
2 eggs, slightly beaten
1/2 C. vegetable oil

Preheat the oven to 400°F. In a large bowl, combine the Holiday Muffin Mix with the water, eggs, and oil. Stir until the mixture is just blended. Do not overmix. Spoon the batter into greased muffin tins, filling 2/3 to 3/4 full. Bake for 15 to 18 minutes, or until golden brown. Serve warm or cool completely on a wire rack.

Variation:

Add 1 cup miniature chocolate chips or 1 cup pecan pieces to the batter.

Holiday Muffins

| 1 jar Holiday Muffin Mix | 2 eggs, slightly beaten |
| 1 1/3 C. water | 1/2 C. vegetable oil |

Preheat the oven to 400°F. In a large bowl, combine the Holiday Muffin Mix with the water, eggs, and oil. Stir until the mixture is just blended. Do not overmix. Spoon the batter into greased muffin tins, filling 2/3 to 3/4 full. Bake for 15 to 18 minutes, or until golden brown. Serve warm or cool completely on a wire rack.

Variation:

Add 1 cup miniature chocolate chips or 1 cup pecan pieces to the batter.

Holiday Muffins

| 1 jar Holiday Muffin Mix | 2 eggs, slightly beaten |
| 1 1/3 C. water | 1/2 C. vegetable oil |

Preheat the oven to 400°F. In a large bowl, combine the Holiday Muffin Mix with the water, eggs, and oil. Stir until the mixture is just blended. Do not overmix. Spoon the batter into greased muffin tins, filling 2/3 to 3/4 full. Bake for 15 to 18 minutes, or until golden brown. Serve warm or cool completely on a wire rack.

Variation:

Add 1 cup miniature chocolate chips or 1 cup pecan pieces to the batter.

Holiday Muffins

| 1 jar Holiday Muffin Mix | 2 eggs, slightly beaten |
| 1 1/3 C. water | 1/2 C. vegetable oil |

Preheat the oven to 400°F. In a large bowl, combine the Holiday Muffin Mix with the water, eggs, and oil. Stir until the mixture is just blended. Do not overmix. Spoon the batter into greased muffin tins, filling 2/3 to 3/4 full. Bake for 15 to 18 minutes, or until golden brown. Serve warm or cool completely on a wire rack.

Variation:

Add 1 cup miniature chocolate chips or 1 cup pecan pieces to the batter.

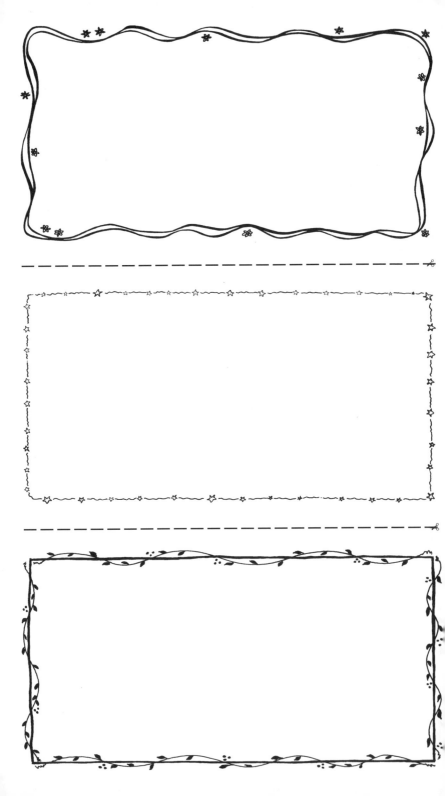

Holiday Muffins

1 jar Holiday Muffin Mix
1 1/3 C . water

2 eggs, slightly beaten
1/2 C. vegetable oil

Preheat the oven to 400°F. In a large bowl, combine the Holiday Muffin Mix with the water, eggs, and oil. Stir until the mixture is just blended. Do not overmix. Spoon the batter into greased muffin tins, filling 2/3 to 3/4 full. Bake for 15 to 18 minutes, or until golden brown. Serve warm or cool completely on a wire rack.

Variation:

Add 1 cup miniature chocolate chips or 1 cup pecan pieces to the batter.

Holiday Muffins

1 jar Holiday Muffin Mix
1 1/3 C . water

2 eggs, slightly beaten
1/2 C. vegetable oil

Preheat the oven to 400°F. In a large bowl, combine the Holiday Muffin Mix with the water, eggs, and oil. Stir until the mixture is just blended. Do not overmix. Spoon the batter into greased muffin tins, filling 2/3 to 3/4 full. Bake for 15 to 18 minutes, or until golden brown. Serve warm or cool completely on a wire rack.

Variation:

Add 1 cup miniature chocolate chips or 1 cup pecan pieces to the batter.

Holiday Muffins

1 jar Holiday Muffin Mix
1 1/3 C . water

2 eggs, slightly beaten
1/2 C. vegetable oil

Preheat the oven to 400°F. In a large bowl, combine the Holiday Muffin Mix with the water, eggs, and oil. Stir until the mixture is just blended. Do not overmix. Spoon the batter into greased muffin tins, filling 2/3 to 3/4 full. Bake for 15 to 18 minutes, or until golden brown. Serve warm or cool completely on a wire rack.

Variation:

Add 1 cup miniature chocolate chips or 1 cup pecan pieces to the batter.

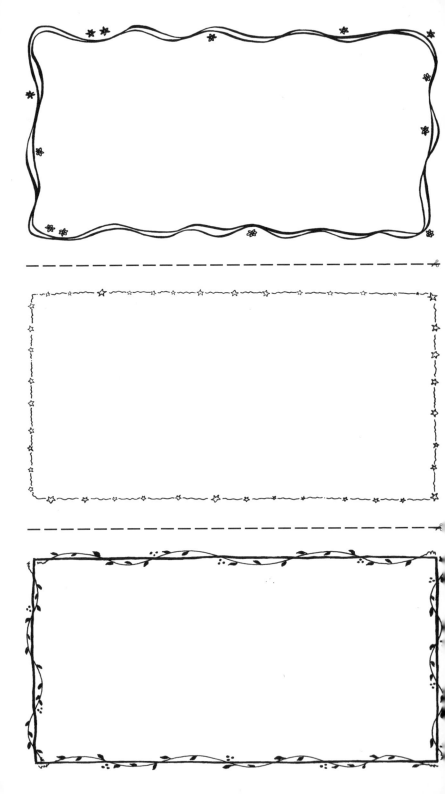

Scone Mix

4 C. all-purpose flour
1 tsp. baking soda
2 tsp. salt
4 tsp. cream of tartar

Layer the ingredients in the order given into a wide-mouth 1-quart canning jar. Pack each layer in place before adding the next ingredient.

Attach a gift tag with the mixing and baking directions.

Scones

1 jar Scone Mix
6 T. butter or margarine,
 softened
1 C. buttermilk
2 eggs, slightly beaten

Preheat the oven to 375°F. In a large bowl, place the Scone Mix. Blend in the butter until it is well distributed. Stir in the buttermilk and eggs. Turn out onto a floured board, and knead for 1 minute. Divide the dough into four pieces. Flatten each piece of dough into a round, 6 inches in diameter and 1/2 inch thick. Cut each circle into 4 pieces. Place on a greased cookie sheet. Bake for 15 minutes, or until golden brown. Serve warm or cool completely on a wire rack.

Scones

1 jar Scone Mix
6 T. butter or margarine,
  softened

1 C. buttermilk
2 eggs, slightly beaten

Preheat the oven to 375°F. In a large bowl, place the Scone Mix. Blend in the butter until it is well distributed. Stir in the buttermilk and eggs. Turn out onto a floured board, and knead for 1 minute. Divide the dough into four pieces. Flatten each piece of dough into a round, 6 inches in diameter and 1/2 inch thick. Cut each circle into 4 pieces. Place on a greased cookie sheet. Bake for 15 minutes, or until golden brown. Serve warm or cool completely on a wire rack.

Scones

1 jar Scone Mix
6 T. butter or margarine,
  softened

1 C. buttermilk
2 eggs, slightly beaten

Preheat the oven to 375°F. In a large bowl, place the Scone Mix. Blend in the butter until it is well distributed. Stir in the buttermilk and eggs. Turn out onto a floured board, and knead for 1 minute. Divide the dough into four pieces. Flatten each piece of dough into a round, 6 inches in diameter and 1/2 inch thick. Cut each circle into 4 pieces. Place on a greased cookie sheet. Bake for 15 minutes, or until golden brown. Serve warm or cool completely on a wire rack.

Scones

1 jar Scone Mix
6 T. butter or margarine,
  softened

1 C. buttermilk
2 eggs, slightly beaten

Preheat the oven to 375°F. In a large bowl, place the Scone Mix. Blend in the butter until it is well distributed. Stir in the buttermilk and eggs. Turn out onto a floured board, and knead for 1 minute. Divide the dough into four pieces. Flatten each piece of dough into a round, 6 inches in diameter and 1/2 inch thick. Cut each circle into 4 pieces. Place on a greased cookie sheet. Bake for 15 minutes, or until golden brown. Serve warm or cool completely on a wire rack.

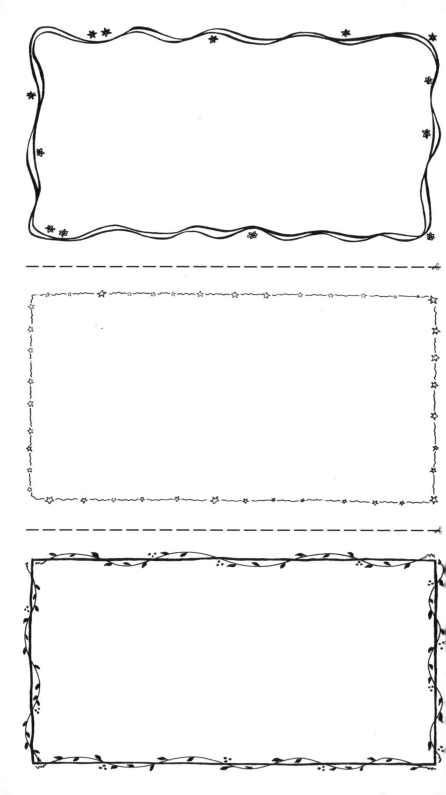

Scones

1 jar Scone Mix
6 T. butter or margarine,
  softened

1 C. buttermilk
2 eggs, slightly beaten

Preheat the oven to 375°F. In a large bowl, place the Scone Mix. Blend in the butter until it is well distributed. Stir in the buttermilk and eggs. Turn out onto a floured board, and knead for 1 minute. Divide the dough into four pieces. Flatten each piece of dough into a round, 6 inches in diameter and 1/2 inch thick. Cut each circle into 4 pieces. Place on a greased cookie sheet. Bake for 15 minutes, or until golden brown. Serve warm or cool completely on a wire rack.

Scones

1 jar Scone Mix
6 T. butter or margarine,
  softened

1 C. buttermilk
2 eggs, slightly beaten

Preheat the oven to 375°F. In a large bowl, place the Scone Mix. Blend in the butter until it is well distributed. Stir in the buttermilk and eggs. Turn out onto a floured board, and knead for 1 minute. Divide the dough into four pieces. Flatten each piece of dough into a round, 6 inches in diameter and 1/2 inch thick. Cut each circle into 4 pieces. Place on a greased cookie sheet. Bake for 15 minutes, or until golden brown. Serve warm or cool completely on a wire rack.

Scones

1 jar Scone Mix
6 T. butter or margarine,
  softened

1 C. buttermilk
2 eggs, slightly beaten

Preheat the oven to 375°F. In a large bowl, place the Scone Mix. Blend in the butter until it is well distributed. Stir in the buttermilk and eggs. Turn out onto a floured board, and knead for 1 minute. Divide the dough into four pieces. Flatten each piece of dough into a round, 6 inches in diameter and 1/2 inch thick. Cut each circle into 4 pieces. Place on a greased cookie sheet. Bake for 15 minutes, or until golden brown. Serve warm or cool completely on a wire rack.

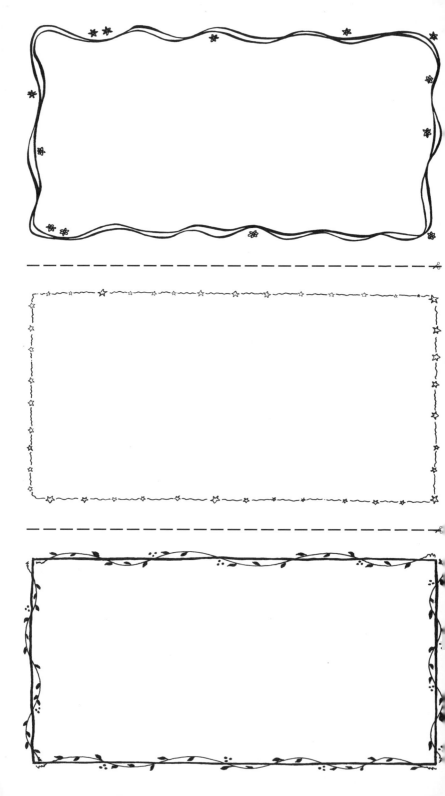

Cornbread Mix

1 C. yellow cornmeal
2 1/2 C. Bisquick baking mix
1/2 C. sugar
1 T. + 1 tsp. baking powder

Layer the ingredients in the order given into a wide-mouth 1-quart canning jar. Pack each layer in place before adding the next ingredient.

Attach a gift tag with the mixing and baking directions.

❀ For a different look, place a small amount of stuffing under a fabric cover before attaching to "puff" the top. ❀

Cornbread

1 jar Cornbread Mix
3 eggs, slightly beaten
1 1/4 C. milk
3/4 C. butter or margarine,
   softened

Preheat the oven to 350°F. In a large bowl, combine the Cornbread Mix with the eggs, milk and butter. Stir until the mixture is just blended. Do not overmix. Divide batter into 2 equal portions, pouring into greased 8-inch round baking pans. Bake for 25 to 30 minutes, or until golden brown. Serve warm or cool completely on a wire rack.

Cornbread

1 jar Cornbread Mix
3 eggs, slightly beaten

1 1/4 C. milk
3/4 C. butter or margarine,
softened

Preheat the oven to 350°F. In a large bowl, combine the Cornbread Mix with the eggs, milk and butter. Stir until the mixture is just blended. Do not overmix. Divide batter into 2 equal portions, pouring into greased 8-inch round baking pans. Bake for 25 to 30 minutes, or until golden brown. Serve warm or cool completely on a wire rack.

Cornbread

1 jar Cornbread Mix
3 eggs, slightly beaten

1 1/4 C. milk
3/4 C. butter or margarine,
softened

Preheat the oven to 350°F. In a large bowl, combine the Cornbread Mix with the eggs, milk and butter. Stir until the mixture is just blended. Do not overmix. Divide batter into 2 equal portions, pouring into greased 8-inch round baking pans. Bake for 25 to 30 minutes, or until golden brown. Serve warm or cool completely on a wire rack.

Cornbread

1 jar Cornbread Mix
3 eggs, slightly beaten

1 1/4 C. milk
3/4 C. butter or margarine,
softened

Preheat the oven to 350°F. In a large bowl, combine the Cornbread Mix with the eggs, milk and butter. Stir until the mixture is just blended. Do not overmix. Divide batter into 2 equal portions, pouring into greased 8-inch round baking pans. Bake for 25 to 30 minutes, or until golden brown. Serve warm or cool completely on a wire rack.

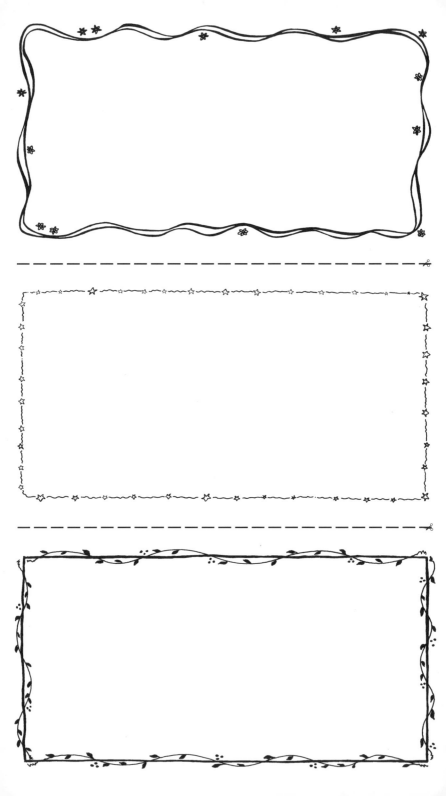

Cornbread

1 jar Cornbread Mix
3 eggs, slightly beaten

1 1/4 C. milk
3/4 C. butter or margarine,
softened

Preheat the oven to 350°F. In a large bowl, combine the Cornbread Mix with the eggs, milk and butter. Stir until the mixture is just blended. Do not overmix. Divide batter into 2 equal portions, pouring into greased 8-inch round baking pans. Bake for 25 to 30 minutes, or until golden brown. Serve warm or cool completely on a wire rack.

Cornbread

1 jar Cornbread Mix
3 eggs, slightly beaten

1 1/4 C. milk
3/4 C. butter or margarine,
softened

Preheat the oven to 350°F. In a large bowl, combine the Cornbread Mix with the eggs, milk and butter. Stir until the mixture is just blended. Do not overmix. Divide batter into 2 equal portions, pouring into greased 8-inch round baking pans. Bake for 25 to 30 minutes, or until golden brown. Serve warm or cool completely on a wire rack.

Cornbread

1 jar Cornbread Mix
3 eggs, slightly beaten

1 1/4 C. milk
3/4 C. butter or margarine,
softened

Preheat the oven to 350°F. In a large bowl, combine the Cornbread Mix with the eggs, milk and butter. Stir until the mixture is just blended. Do not overmix. Divide batter into 2 equal portions, pouring into greased 8-inch round baking pans. Bake for 25 to 30 minutes, or until golden brown. Serve warm or cool completely on a wire rack.

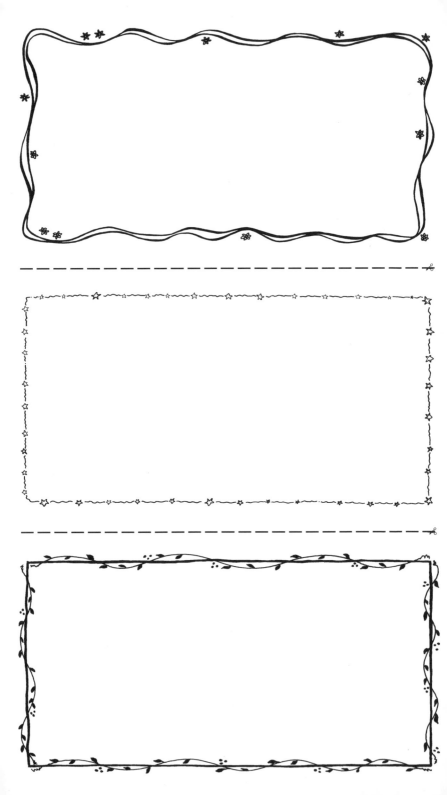

Cherry Bread Mix

1/2 C. nuts
1/2 C. dried cherries, finely
   chopped
1/2 C. sugar
2 1/2 C. Bisquick
1 tsp. baking powder
1/4 tsp. salt

Layer the ingredients in the order given into a wide-mouth 1-quart canning jar. Pack each layer in place before adding the next ingredient.

Attach a gift tag with the mixing and baking directions.

Cherry Bread

1 jar Cherry Bread Mix
1/2 C. butter or margarine,
    softened
2 eggs, slightly beaten
1 1/4 C. milk
1 tsp. vanilla

Preheat the oven to 350°F. In a large bowl, place the Cherry Bread Mix. Make a well in the center. Mix wet ingredients and pour into dry mixture. Stir until the mixture is blended. Spoon the batter into a large loaf pan that is well greased with waxed paper in the bottom. Bake for 1 hour or until knife inserted in the center comes out clean. Cool in the pan on a wire rack before removing.

Cherry Bread

1 jar Cherry Bread Mix	2 eggs, slightly beaten
1/2 C. butter or margarine,	1 1/4 C. milk
softened	1 tsp. vanilla

Preheat the oven to 350°F. In a large bowl, place the Cherry Bread Mix. Make a well in the center. Mix wet ingredients and pour into dry mixture. Stir until the mixture is blended. Spoon the batter into a large loaf pan that is well greased with waxed paper in the bottom. Bake for 1 hour or until knife inserted in the center comes out clean. Cool in the pan on a wire rack before removing.

Cherry Bread

1 jar Cherry Bread Mix	2 eggs, slightly beaten
1/2 C. butter or margarine,	1 1/4 C. milk
softened	1 tsp. vanilla

Preheat the oven to 350°F. In a large bowl, place the Cherry Bread Mix. Make a well in the center. Mix wet ingredients and pour into dry mixture. Stir until the mixture is blended. Spoon the batter into a large loaf pan that is well greased with waxed paper in the bottom. Bake for 1 hour or until knife inserted in the center comes out clean. Cool in the pan on a wire rack before removing.

Cherry Bread

1 jar Cherry Bread Mix	2 eggs, slightly beaten
1/2 C. butter or margarine,	1 1/4 C. milk
softened	1 tsp. vanilla

Preheat the oven to 350°F. In a large bowl, place the Cherry Bread Mix. Make a well in the center. Mix wet ingredients and pour into dry mixture. Stir until the mixture is blended. Spoon the batter into a large loaf pan that is well greased with waxed paper in the bottom. Bake for 1 hour or until knife inserted in the center comes out clean. Cool in the pan on a wire rack before.removing.

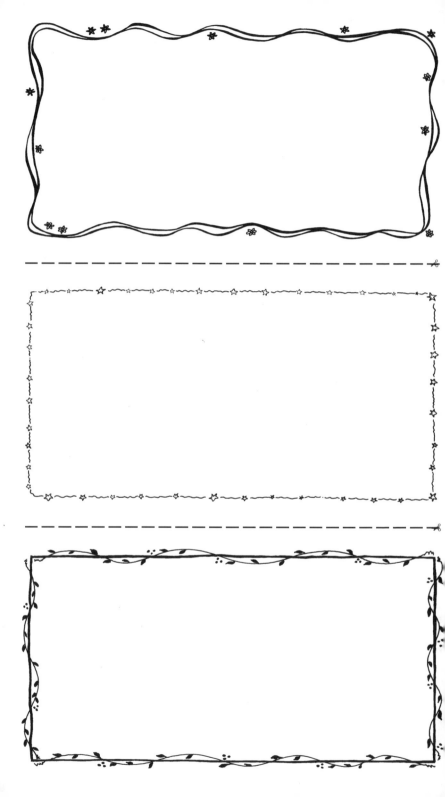

Cherry Bread

1 jar Cherry Bread Mix
1/2 C. butter or margarine,
  softened

2 eggs, slightly beaten
1 1/4 C. milk
1 tsp. vanilla

Preheat the oven to 350°F. In a large bowl, place the Cherry Bread Mix. Make a well in the center. Mix wet ingredients and pour into dry mixture. Stir until the mixture is blended. Spoon the batter into a large loaf pan that is well greased with waxed paper in the bottom. Bake for 1 hour or until knife inserted in the center comes out clean. Cool in the pan on a wire rack before removing.

Cherry Bread

1 jar Cherry Bread Mix
1/2 C. butter or margarine,
  softened

2 eggs, slightly beaten
1 1/4 C. milk
1 tsp. vanilla

Preheat the oven to 350°F. In a large bowl, place the Cherry Bread Mix. Make a well in the center. Mix wet ingredients and pour into dry mixture. Stir until the mixture is blended. Spoon the batter into a large loaf pan that is well greased with waxed paper in the bottom. Bake for 1 hour or until knife inserted in the center comes out clean. Cool in the pan on a wire rack before removing.

Cherry Bread

1 jar Cherry Bread Mix
1/2 C. butter or margarine,
  softened

2 eggs, slightly beaten
1 1/4 C. milk
1 tsp. vanilla

Preheat the oven to 350°F. In a large bowl, place the Cherry Bread Mix. Make a well in the center. Mix wet ingredients and pour into dry mixture. Stir until the mixture is blended. Spoon the batter into a large loaf pan that is well greased with waxed paper in the bottom. Bake for 1 hour or until knife inserted in the center comes out clean. Cool in the pan on a wire rack before removing.

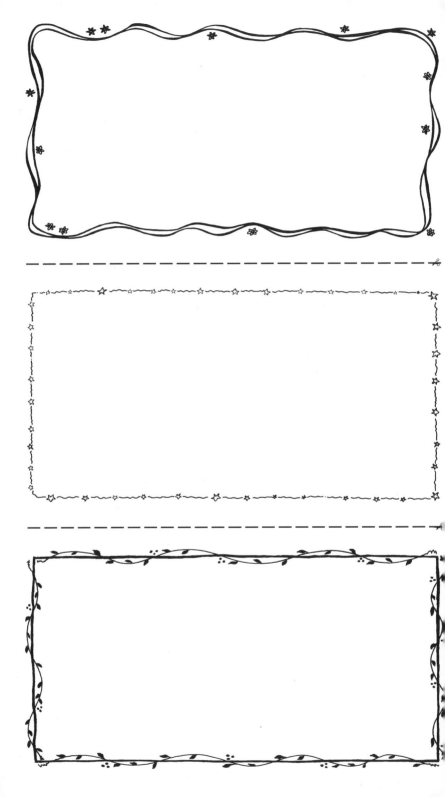

Pumpkin Bread Mix

3 C. Bisquick
1 C. sugar
1 tsp. pumpkin pie spice
1/2 tsp. nutmeg
1/2 tsp. ground cloves

Layer the ingredients in the order given into a wide-mouth 1-quart canning jar. Pack each layer in place before adding the next ingredient.

Attach a gift tag with the mixing and baking directions.

❋ *At times, it may seem impossible to make all of the jar ingredients fit, but with persistence, they do all fit.* ❋

Pumpkin Bread

1 jar Pumpkin Bread Mix
1 (16 oz.) can solid pack pumpkin
2 eggs, slightly beaten
1 C. chopped nuts

Preheat the oven to 350°F. In a large bowl, combine the Pumpkin Bread Mix with the pumpkin, eggs and nuts. Stir until the mixture is blended. Spoon the batter into either 1 large greased loaf pan or 2 small greased loaf pans. Bake 1 large loaf for 1 hour or 2 small loaves for 45 minutes. Cool in the pan on a wire rack before removing.

Pumpkin Bread

1 jar Pumpkin Bread Mix
1 (16 oz.) can solid pack
  pumpkin

2 eggs, slightly beaten
1 C. chopped nuts

    Preheat the oven to 350°F. In a large bowl, combine the Pumpkin Bread Mix with the pumpkin, eggs and nuts. Stir until the mixture is blended. Spoon the batter into either 1 large greased loaf pan or 2 small greased loaf pans. Bake 1 large loaf for 1 hour or 2 small loaves for 45 minutes. Cool in the pan on a wire rack before removing.

Pumpkin Bread

1 jar Pumpkin Bread Mix
1 (16 oz.) can solid pack
  pumpkin

2 eggs, slightly beaten
1 C. chopped nuts

    Preheat the oven to 350°F. In a large bowl, combine the Pumpkin Bread Mix with the pumpkin, eggs and nuts. Stir until the mixture is blended. Spoon the batter into either 1 large greased loaf pan or 2 small greased loaf pans. Bake 1 large loaf for 1 hour or 2 small loaves for 45 minutes. Cool in the pan on a wire rack before removing.

Pumpkin Bread

1 jar Pumpkin Bread Mix
1 (16 oz.) can solid pack
  pumpkin

2 eggs, slightly beaten
1 C. chopped nuts

    Preheat the oven to 350°F. In a large bowl, combine the Pumpkin Bread Mix with the pumpkin, eggs and nuts. Stir until the mixture is blended. Spoon the batter into either 1 large greased loaf pan or 2 small greased loaf pans. Bake 1 large loaf for 1 hour or 2 small loaves for 45 minutes. Cool in the pan on a wire rack before removing.

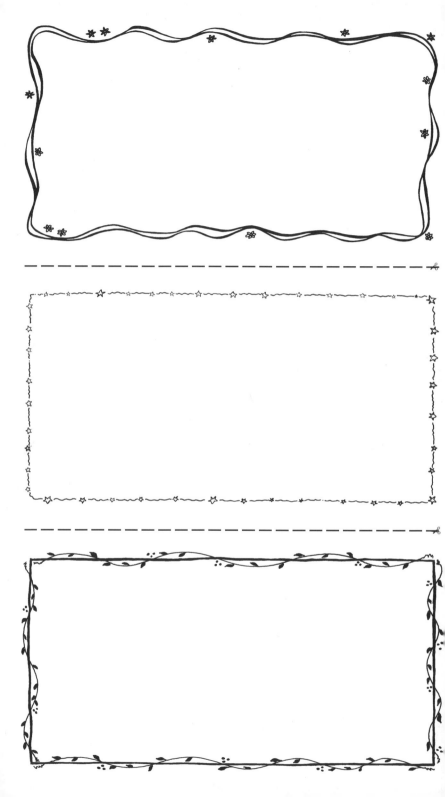

Pumpkin Bread

1 jar Pumpkin Bread Mix
1 (16 oz.) can solid pack
  pumpkin

2 eggs, slightly beaten
1 C. chopped nuts

Preheat the oven to 350°F. In a large bowl, combine the Pumpkin Bread Mix with the pumpkin, eggs and nuts. Stir until the mixture is blended. Spoon the batter into either 1 large greased loaf pan or 2 small greased loaf pans. Bake 1 large loaf for 1 hour or 2 small loaves for 45 minutes. Cool in the pan on a wire rack before removing.

Pumpkin Bread

1 jar Pumpkin Bread Mix
1 (16 oz.) can solid pack
  pumpkin

2 eggs, slightly beaten
1 C. chopped nuts

Preheat the oven to 350°F. In a large bowl, combine the Pumpkin Bread Mix with the pumpkin, eggs and nuts. Stir until the mixture is blended. Spoon the batter into either 1 large greased loaf pan or 2 small greased loaf pans. Bake 1 large loaf for 1 hour or 2 small loaves for 45 minutes. Cool in the pan on a wire rack before removing.

Pumpkin Bread

1 jar Pumpkin Bread Mix
1 (16 oz.) can solid pack
  pumpkin

2 eggs, slightly beaten
1 C. chopped nuts

Preheat the oven to 350°F. In a large bowl, combine the Pumpkin Bread Mix with the pumpkin, eggs and nuts. Stir until the mixture is blended. Spoon the batter into either 1 large greased loaf pan or 2 small greased loaf pans. Bake 1 large loaf for 1 hour or 2 small loaves for 45 minutes. Cool in the pan on a wire rack before removing.

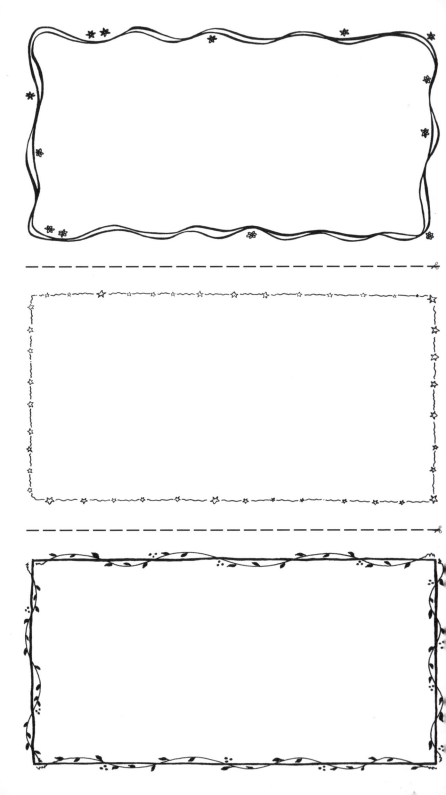

Peach Bread Mix

1/2 C. nuts
1/2 C. dried peaches,
   finely chopped
1/2 C. sugar
2 1/2 C. Bisquick
1 tsp. baking powder
1/4 tsp. salt

Layer the ingredients in the order given into a wide-mouth 1-quart canning jar. Pack each layer in place before adding the next ingredient.

Attach a gift tag with the mixing and baking directions.

Peach Bread

1 jar Peach Bread Mix
1/2 C. butter or margarine,
  softened
2 eggs, slightly beaten
1 1/4 C. milk
1 tsp. vanilla

Preheat the oven to 350°F. In a large bowl, place the Peach Bread Mix. Make a well in the center. Mix wet ingredients and pour into dry mixture. Stir until the mixture is blended. Spoon the batter into a large loaf pan that is well greased with waxed paper in the bottom. Bake for 1 hour or until knife inserted in the center comes out clean. Cool in the pan on a wire rack before removing.

Peach Bread

1 jar Peach Bread Mix
1/2 C. butter or margarine,
  softened

2 eggs, slightly beaten
1 1/4 C. milk
1 tsp. vanilla

Preheat the oven to 350°F. In a large bowl, place the Peach Bread Mix. Make a well in the center. Mix wet ingredients and pour into dry mixture. Stir until the mixture is blended. Spoon the batter into a large loaf pan that is well greased with waxed paper in the bottom. Bake for 1 hour or until knife inserted in the center comes out clean. Cool in the pan on a wire rack before removing.

Peach Bread

1 jar Peach Bread Mix
1/2 C. butter or margarine,
  softened

2 eggs, slightly beaten
1 1/4 C. milk
1 tsp. vanilla

Preheat the oven to 350°F. In a large bowl, place the Peach Bread Mix. Make a well in the center. Mix wet ingredients and pour into dry mixture. Stir until the mixture is blended. Spoon the batter into a large loaf pan that is well greased with waxed paper in the bottom. Bake for 1 hour or until knife inserted in the center comes out clean. Cool in the pan on a wire rack before removing.

Peach Bread

1 jar Peach Bread Mix
1/2 C. butter or margarine,
  softened

2 eggs, slightly beaten
1 1/4 C. milk
1 tsp. vanilla

Preheat the oven to 350°F. In a large bowl, place the Peach Bread Mix. Make a well in the center. Mix wet ingredients and pour into dry mixture. Stir until the mixture is blended. Spoon the batter into a large loaf pan that is well greased with waxed paper in the bottom. Bake for 1 hour or until knife inserted in the center comes out clean. Cool in the pan on a wire rack before removing.

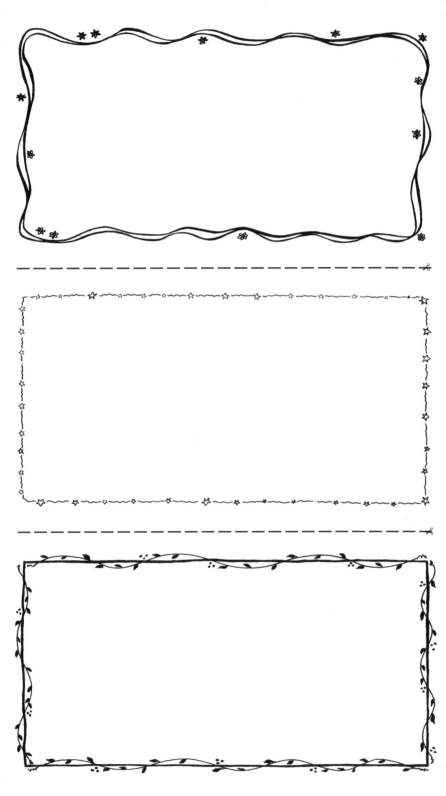

Peach Bread

1 jar Peach Bread Mix
1/2 C. butter or margarine,
  softened

2 eggs, slightly beaten
1 1/4 C. milk
1 tsp. vanilla

Preheat the oven to 350°F. In a large bowl, place the Peach Bread Mix. Make a well in the center. Mix wet ingredients and pour into dry mixture. Stir until the mixture is blended. Spoon the batter into a large loaf pan that is well greased with waxed paper in the bottom. Bake for 1 hour or until knife inserted in the center comes out clean. Cool in the pan on a wire rack before removing.

Peach Bread

1 jar Peach Bread Mix
1/2 C. butter or margarine,
  softened

2 eggs, slightly beaten
1 1/4 C. milk
1 tsp. vanilla

Preheat the oven to 350°F. In a large bowl, place the Peach Bread Mix. Make a well in the center. Mix wet ingredients and pour into dry mixture. Stir until the mixture is blended. Spoon the batter into a large loaf pan that is well greased with waxed paper in the bottom. Bake for 1 hour or until knife inserted in the center comes out clean. Cool in the pan on a wire rack before removing.

Peach Bread

1 jar Peach Bread Mix
1/2 C. butter or margarine,
  softened

2 eggs, slightly beaten
1 1/4 C. milk
1 tsp. vanilla

Preheat the oven to 350°F. In a large bowl, place the Peach Bread Mix. Make a well in the center. Mix wet ingredients and pour into dry mixture. Stir until the mixture is blended. Spoon the batter into a large loaf pan that is well greased with waxed paper in the bottom. Bake for 1 hour or until knife inserted in the center comes out clean. Cool in the pan on a wire rack before removing.

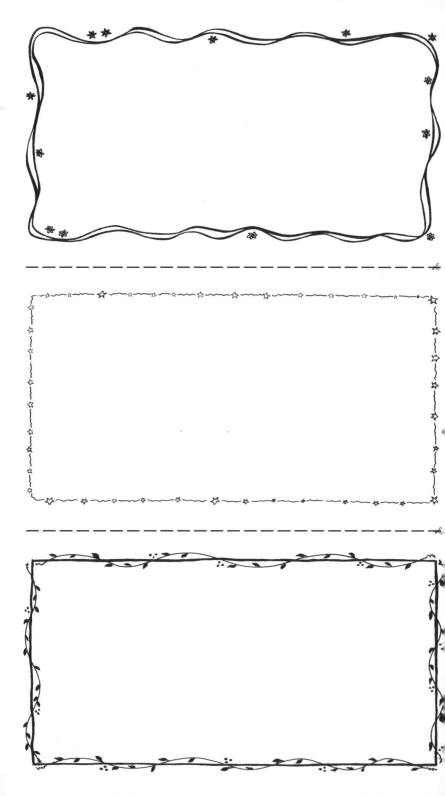

Strawberry Bread Mix

3 C. all-purpose flour
1 tsp. baking soda
1 tsp. salt
2 1/2 tsp. cinnamon
1 C. sugar

Layer the ingredients in the order given into a wide-mouth 1-quart canning jar. Pack each layer in place before adding the next ingredient.

Attach a gift tag with the mixing and baking directions.

❀ *Small appliques or embroidery can be added to the center of a fabric cover to further personalize the gift.* ❀

Strawberry Bread

1 jar Strawberry Bread Mix
20 oz. frozen strawberries,
   thawed slightly
4 eggs, slightly beaten
1 1/4 C. oil

Preheat the oven to 350°F. In a large bowl, place the Strawberry Bread Mix. Make a well in the center. Mix wet ingredients and pour into dry mixture. Stir until the mixture is blended. Spoon the batter into either 2 large greased loaf pans or 4 small greased loaf pans. Bake large loaves for 1 hour or small loaves for 45 minutes. Cool in the pan on a wire rack before removing.

Strawberry Bread

1 jar Strawberry Bread Mix
20 oz. frozen strawberries,
  thawed slightly

4 eggs, slightly beaten
1 1/4 C. oil

Preheat the oven to 350°F. In a large bowl, place the Strawberry Bread Mix. Make a well in the center. Mix wet ingredients and pour into dry mixture. Stir until the mixture is blended. Spoon the batter into either 2 large greased loaf pans or 4 small greased loaf pans. Bake large loaves for 1 hour or small loaves for 45 minutes. Cool in the pan on a wire rack before removing.

Strawberry Bread

1 jar Strawberry Bread Mix
20 oz. frozen strawberries,
  thawed slightly

4 eggs, slightly beaten
1 1/4 C. oil

Preheat the oven to 350°F. In a large bowl, place the Strawberry Bread Mix. Make a well in the center. Mix wet ingredients and pour into dry mixture. Stir until the mixture is blended. Spoon the batter into either 2 large greased loaf pans or 4 small greased loaf pans. Bake large loaves for 1 hour or small loaves for 45 minutes. Cool in the pan on a wire rack before removing.

Strawberry Bread

1 jar Strawberry Bread Mix
20 oz. frozen strawberries,
  thawed slightly

4 eggs, slightly beaten
1 1/4 C. oil

Preheat the oven to 350°F. In a large bowl, place the Strawberry Bread Mix. Make a well in the center. Mix wet ingredients and pour into dry mixture. Stir until the mixture is blended. Spoon the batter into either 2 large greased loaf pans or 4 small greased loaf pans. Bake large loaves for 1 hour or small loaves for 45 minutes. Cool in the pan on a wire rack before removing.

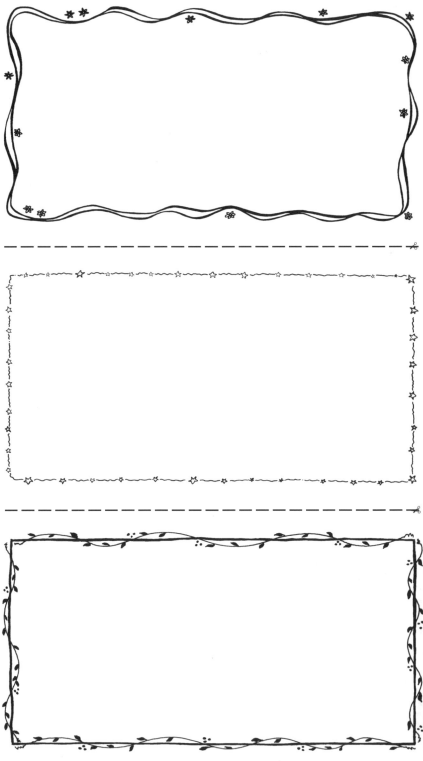

Strawberry Bread

1 jar Strawberry Bread Mix
20 oz. frozen strawberries,
   thawed slightly

4 eggs, slightly beaten
1 1/4 C. oil

Preheat the oven to 350°F. In a large bowl, place the Strawberry Bread Mix. Make a well in the center. Mix wet ingredients and pour into dry mixture. Stir until the mixture is blended. Spoon the batter into either 2 large greased loaf pans or 4 small greased loaf pans. Bake large loaves for 1 hour or small loaves for 45 minutes. Cool in the pan on a wire rack before removing.

Strawberry Bread

1 jar Strawberry Bread Mix
20 oz. frozen strawberries,
   thawed slightly

4 eggs, slightly beaten
1 1/4 C. oil

Preheat the oven to 350°F. In a large bowl, place the Strawberry Bread Mix. Make a well in the center. Mix wet ingredients and pour into dry mixture. Stir until the mixture is blended. Spoon the batter into either 2 large greased loaf pans or 4 small greased loaf pans. Bake large loaves for 1 hour or small loaves for 45 minutes. Cool in the pan on a wire rack before removing.

Strawberry Bread

1 jar Strawberry Bread Mix
20 oz. frozen strawberries,
   thawed slightly

4 eggs, slightly beaten
1 1/4 C. oil

Preheat the oven to 350°F. In a large bowl, place the Strawberry Bread Mix. Make a well in the center. Mix wet ingredients and pour into dry mixture. Stir until the mixture is blended. Spoon the batter into either 2 large greased loaf pans or 4 small greased loaf pans. Bake large loaves for 1 hour or small loaves for 45 minutes. Cool in the pan on a wire rack before removing.

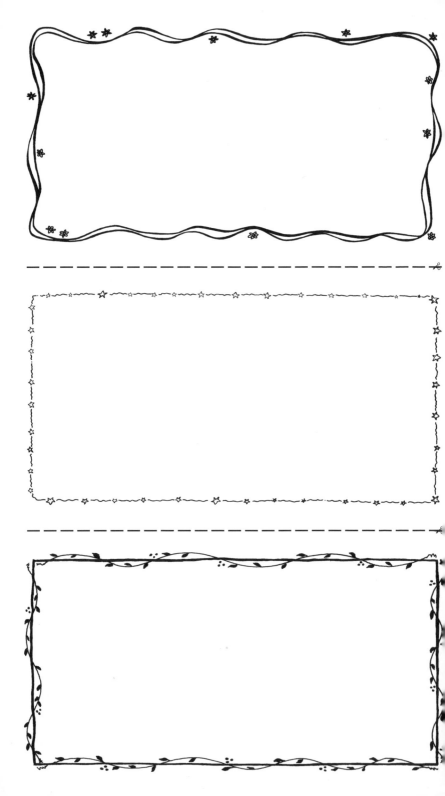

Apricot Bread Mix

1/2 C. nuts
1/2 C. dried apricots,
  finely chopped
1/2 C. sugar
2 1/2 C. Bisquick
1 tsp. baking powder
1/4 tsp. salt

Layer the ingredients in the order given into a wide-mouth 1-quart canning jar. Pack each layer in place before adding the next ingredient.

Attach a gift tag with the mixing and baking directions.

Apricot Bread

1 jar Apricot Bread Mix
1/2 C. butter or margarine,
    softened
2 eggs, slightly beaten
1 1/4 C. milk
1 tsp. vanilla

Preheat the oven to 350°F. In a large bowl, place the Apricot Bread Mix. Make a well in the center. Mix wet ingredients and pour into dry mixture. Stir until the mixture is blended. Spoon the batter into a large loaf pan that is well greased with waxed paper in the bottom. Bake for 1 hour or until knife inserted in the center comes out clean. Cool in the pan on a wire rack before removing.

Apricot Bread

1 jar Apricot Bread Mix
1/2 C. butter or margarine,
  softened

2 eggs, slightly beaten
1 1/4 C. milk
1 tsp. vanilla

Preheat the oven to 350°F. In a large bowl, place the Apricot Bread Mix. Make a well in the center. Mix wet ingredients and pour into dry mixture. Stir until the mixture is blended. Spoon the batter into a large loaf pan that is well greased with waxed paper in the bottom. Bake for 1 hour or until knife inserted in the center comes out clean. Cool in the pan on a wire rack before removing.

Apricot Bread

1 jar Apricot Bread Mix
1/2 C. butter or margarine,
  softened

2 eggs, slightly beaten
1 1/4 C. milk
1 tsp. vanilla

Preheat the oven to 350°F. In a large bowl, place the Apricot Bread Mix. Make a well in the center. Mix wet ingredients and pour into dry mixture. Stir until the mixture is blended. Spoon the batter into a large loaf pan that is well greased with waxed paper in the bottom. Bake for 1 hour or until knife inserted in the center comes out clean. Cool in the pan on a wire rack before removing.

Apricot Bread

1 jar Apricot Bread Mix
1/2 C. butter or margarine,
  softened

2 eggs, slightly beaten
1 1/4 C. milk
1 tsp. vanilla

Preheat the oven to 350°F. In a large bowl, place the Apricot Bread Mix. Make a well in the center. Mix wet ingredients and pour into dry mixture. Stir until the mixture is blended. Spoon the batter into a large loaf pan that is well greased with waxed paper in the bottom. Bake for 1 hour or until knife inserted in the center comes out clean. Cool in the pan on a wire rack before removing.

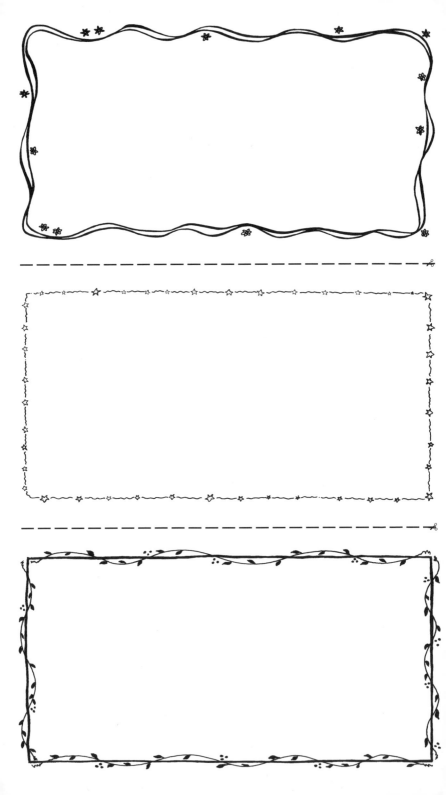

Apricot Bread

1 jar Apricot Bread Mix
1/2 C. butter or margarine,
  softened

2 eggs, slightly beaten
1 1/4 C. milk
1 tsp. vanilla

Preheat the oven to 350°F. In a large bowl, place the Apricot Bread Mix. Make a well in the center. Mix wet ingredients and pour into dry mixture. Stir until the mixture is blended. Spoon the batter into a large loaf pan that is well greased with waxed paper in the bottom. Bake for 1 hour or until knife inserted in the center comes out clean. Cool in the pan on a wire rack before removing.

Apricot Bread

1 jar Apricot Bread Mix
1/2 C. butter or margarine,
  softened

2 eggs, slightly beaten
1 1/4 C. milk
1 tsp. vanilla

Preheat the oven to 350°F. In a large bowl, place the Apricot Bread Mix. Make a well in the center. Mix wet ingredients and pour into dry mixture. Stir until the mixture is blended. Spoon the batter into a large loaf pan that is well greased with waxed paper in the bottom. Bake for 1 hour or until knife inserted in the center comes out clean. Cool in the pan on a wire rack before removing.

Apricot Bread

1 jar Apricot Bread Mix
1/2 C. butter or margarine,
  softened

2 eggs, slightly beaten
1 1/4 C. milk
1 tsp. vanilla

Preheat the oven to 350°F. In a large bowl, place the Apricot Bread Mix. Make a well in the center. Mix wet ingredients and pour into dry mixture. Stir until the mixture is blended. Spoon the batter into a large loaf pan that is well greased with waxed paper in the bottom. Bake for 1 hour or until knife inserted in the center comes out clean. Cool in the pan on a wire rack before removing.

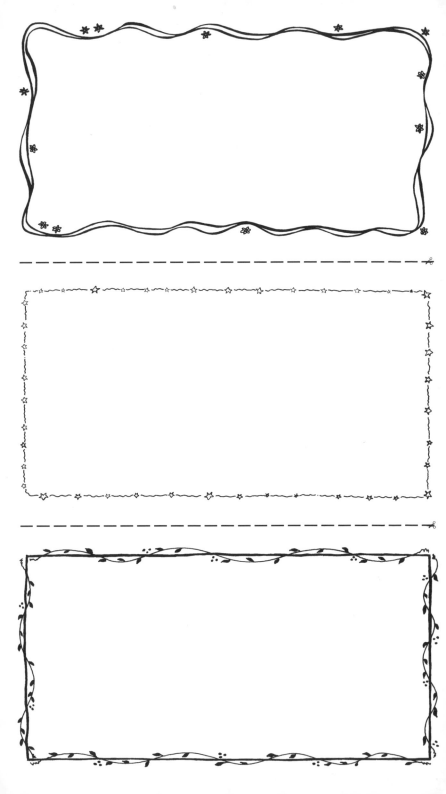

Butter Pecan Bread Mix

1 1/8 C. all-purpose flour
1/2 tsp. cinnamon
1/4 tsp. nutmeg
1/2 C. brown sugar
1 C. chopped pecans
1/2 C. brown sugar
1 1/8 C. all-purpose flour
1/2 tsp. baking soda
1/2 tsp. salt
2 tsp. baking powder

Layer the ingredients in the order given into a wide-mouth 1-quart canning jar. Pack each layer in place before adding the next ingredient.

Attach a gift tag with the mixing and baking directions.

Butter Pecan Bread

1 jar Butter Pecan Bread Mix
1 egg, slightly beaten
1 C. buttermilk
2 T. butter or margarine,
   softened

Preheat the oven to 350°F. In a large bowl, combine the Butter Pecan Bread Mix with the egg, buttermilk and butter. Stir until the mixture is moistened. Spoon the batter into 1 large greased loaf pan. Bake for 1 hour. Cool slightly in the pan on a wire rack before removing.

Butter Pecan Bread

1 jar Butter Pecan Bread Mix
1 egg, slightly beaten

1 C. buttermilk
2 T. butter or margarine, softened

Preheat the oven to 350°F. In a large bowl, combine the Butter Pecan Bread Mix with the egg, buttermilk and butter. Stir until the mixture is moistened. Spoon the batter into 1 large greased loaf pan. Bake for 1 hour. Cool slightly in the pan on a wire rack before removing.

Butter Pecan Bread

1 jar Butter Pecan Bread Mix
1 egg, slightly beaten

1 C. buttermilk
2 T. butter or margarine, softened

Preheat the oven to 350°F. In a large bowl, combine the Butter Pecan Bread Mix with the egg, buttermilk and butter. Stir until the mixture is moistened. Spoon the batter into 1 large greased loaf pan. Bake for 1 hour. Cool slightly in the pan on a wire rack before removing.

Butter Pecan Bread

1 jar Butter Pecan Bread Mix
1 egg, slightly beaten

1 C. buttermilk
2 T. butter or margarine, softened

Preheat the oven to 350°F. In a large bowl, combine the Butter Pecan Bread Mix with the egg, buttermilk and butter. Stir until the mixture is moistened. Spoon the batter into 1 large greased loaf pan. Bake for 1 hour. Cool slightly in the pan on a wire rack before removing.

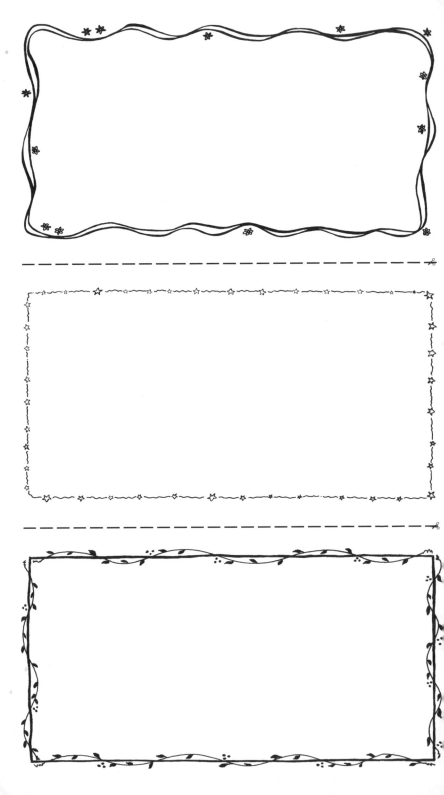

Butter Pecan Bread

1 jar Butter Pecan Bread Mix   1 C. buttermilk
1 egg, slightly beaten   2 T. butter or margarine,
          softened

     Preheat the oven to 350°F. In a large bowl, combine the Butter
Pecan Bread Mix with the egg, buttermilk and butter. Stir until the
mixture is moistened. Spoon the batter into 1 large greased loaf
pan. Bake for 1 hour. Cool slightly in the pan on a wire rack before
removing.

Butter Pecan Bread

1 jar Butter Pecan Bread Mix   1 C. buttermilk
1 egg, slightly beaten   2 T. butter or margarine,
          softened

     Preheat the oven to 350°F. In a large bowl, combine the Butter
Pecan Bread Mix with the egg, buttermilk and butter. Stir until the
mixture is moistened. Spoon the batter into 1 large greased loaf
pan. Bake for 1 hour. Cool slightly in the pan on a wire rack before
removing.

Butter Pecan Bread

1 jar Butter Pecan Bread Mix   1 C. buttermilk
1 egg, slightly beaten   2 T. butter or margarine,
          softened

     Preheat the oven to 350°F. In a large bowl, combine the Butter
Pecan Bread Mix with the egg, buttermilk and butter. Stir until the
mixture is moistened. Spoon the batter into 1 large greased loaf
pan. Bake for 1 hour. Cool slightly in the pan on a wire rack before
removing.

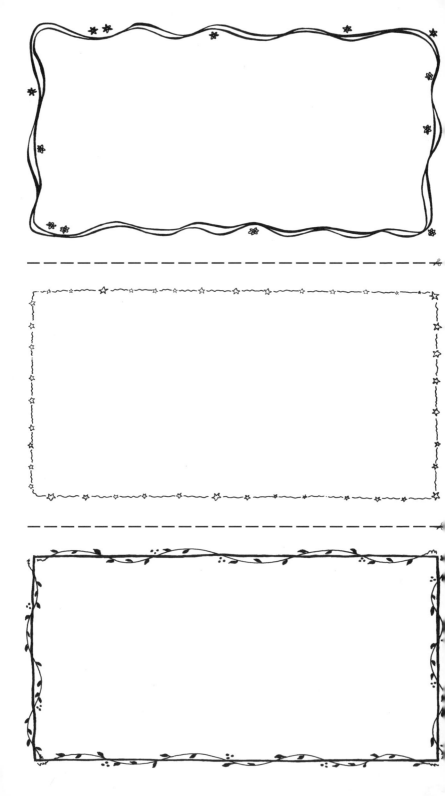

Cranberry Bread Mix

1/2 C. dried orange slices,
  finely chopped
1/2 C. dried cranberries,
  finely chopped
1/2 C. sugar
2 1/2 C. Bisquick
1 tsp. baking powder
1/4 tsp. salt

Layer the ingredients in the order given into a wide-mouth 1-quart canning jar. Pack each layer in place before adding the next ingredient.

Attach a gift tag with the mixing and baking directions.

❋ *For a special touch, attach a wooden spoon to the jar.* ❋

Cranberry Bread

1 jar Cranberry Bread Mix
1/2 C. butter or margarine,
  softened
2 eggs, slightly beaten
1 1/4 C. milk
1 tsp. vanilla

Preheat the oven to 350°F. In a large bowl, place the Cranberry Bread Mix. Make a well in the center. Mix wet ingredients and pour into dry mixture. Stir until the mixture is blended. Spoon the batter into a large loaf pan that is well greased with waxed paper in the bottom. Bake for 1 hour or until knife inserted in the center comes out clean. Cool in the pan on a wire rack before removing.

Cranberry Bread

1 jar Cranberry Bread Mix	2 eggs, slightly beaten
1/2 C. butter or margarine, softened	1 1/4 C. milk
	1 tsp. vanilla

Preheat the oven to 350°F. In a large bowl, place the Cranberry Bread Mix. Make a well in the center. Mix wet ingredients and pour into dry mixture. Stir until the mixture is blended. Spoon the batter into a large loaf pan that is well greased with waxed paper in the bottom. Bake for 1 hour or until knife inserted in the center comes out clean. Cool in the pan on a wire rack before removing.

Cranberry Bread

1 jar Cranberry Bread Mix	2 eggs, slightly beaten
1/2 C. butter or margarine, softened	1 1/4 C. milk
	1 tsp. vanilla

Preheat the oven to 350°F. In a large bowl, place the Cranberry Bread Mix. Make a well in the center. Mix wet ingredients and pour into dry mixture. Stir until the mixture is blended. Spoon the batter into a large loaf pan that is well greased with waxed paper in the bottom. Bake for 1 hour or until knife inserted in the center comes out clean. Cool in the pan on a wire rack before removing.

Cranberry Bread

1 jar Cranberry Bread Mix	2 eggs, slightly beaten
1/2 C. butter or margarine, softened	1 1/4 C. milk
	1 tsp. vanilla

Preheat the oven to 350°F. In a large bowl, place the Cranberry Bread Mix. Make a well in the center. Mix wet ingredients and pour into dry mixture. Stir until the mixture is blended. Spoon the batter into a large loaf pan that is well greased with waxed paper in the bottom. Bake for 1 hour or until knife inserted in the center comes out clean. Cool in the pan on a wire rack before removing.

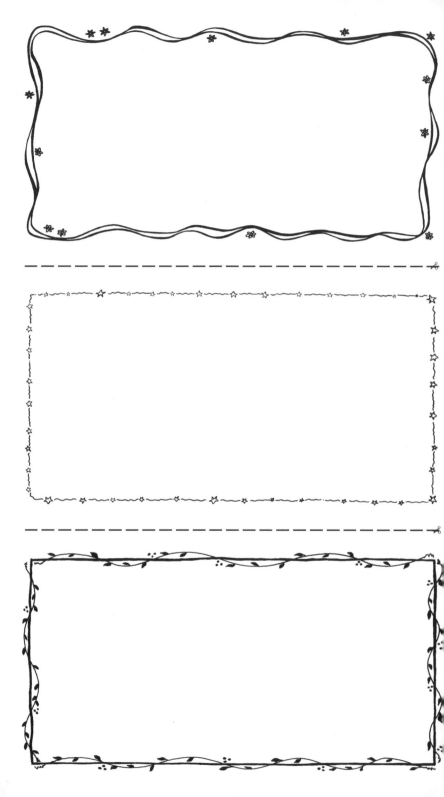

Cranberry Bread

1 jar Cranberry Bread Mix	2 eggs, slightly beaten
1/2 C. butter or margarine, softened	1 1/4 C. milk
	1 tsp. vanilla

Preheat the oven to 350°F. In a large bowl, place the Cranberry Bread Mix. Make a well in the center. Mix wet ingredients and pour into dry mixture. Stir until the mixture is blended. Spoon the batter into a large loaf pan that is well greased with waxed paper in the bottom. Bake for 1 hour or until knife inserted in the center comes out clean. Cool in the pan on a wire rack before removing.

Cranberry Bread

1 jar Cranberry Bread Mix	2 eggs, slightly beaten
1/2 C. butter or margarine, softened	1 1/4 C. milk
	1 tsp. vanilla

Preheat the oven to 350°F. In a large bowl, place the Cranberry Bread Mix. Make a well in the center. Mix wet ingredients and pour into dry mixture. Stir until the mixture is blended. Spoon the batter into a large loaf pan that is well greased with waxed paper in the bottom. Bake for 1 hour or until knife inserted in the center comes out clean. Cool in the pan on a wire rack before removing.

Cranberry Bread

1 jar Cranberry Bread Mix	2 eggs, slightly beaten
1/2 C. butter or margarine, softened	1 1/4 C. milk
	1 tsp. vanilla

Preheat the oven to 350°F. In a large bowl, place the Cranberry Bread Mix. Make a well in the center. Mix wet ingredients and pour into dry mixture. Stir until the mixture is blended. Spoon the batter into a large loaf pan that is well greased with waxed paper in the bottom. Bake for 1 hour or until knife inserted in the center comes out clean. Cool in the pan on a wire rack before removing.

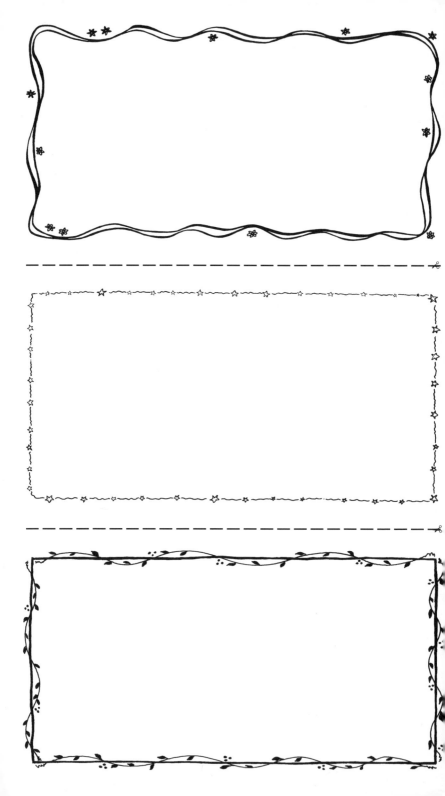

Banana Bread Mix

1/2 C. nuts
1/2 C. finely chopped dried
   bananas
1/2 C. sugar
2 1/2 C. Bisquick
1 tsp. baking powder
1/4 tsp. salt

Layer the ingredients in the order given into a wide-mouth 1-quart canning jar. Pack each layer in place before adding the next ingredient.

Attach a gift tag with the mixing and baking directions.

Banana Bread

1 jar Banana Bread Mix
1/2 C. butter or margarine,
   softened
2 eggs, slightly beaten
1 1/4 C. milk
1 tsp. vanilla

Preheat the oven to 350°F. In a large bowl, place the Banana Bread Mix. Make a well in the center. Mix wet ingredients and pour into dry mixture. Stir until the mixture is blended. Spoon the batter into a large loaf pan that is well greased with waxed paper in the bottom. Bake for 1 hour or until knife inserted in the center comes out clean. Cool in the pan on a wire rack before removing.

Banana Bread

1 jar Banana Bread Mix
1/2 C. butter or margarine,
   softened

2 eggs, slightly beaten
1 1/4 C. milk
1 tsp. vanilla

Preheat the oven to 350°F. In a large bowl, place the Banana Bread Mix. Make a well in the center. Mix wet ingredients and pour into dry mixture. Stir until the mixture is blended. Spoon the batter into a large loaf pan that is well greased with waxed paper in the bottom. Bake for 1 hour or until knife inserted in the center comes out clean. Cool in the pan on a wire rack before removing.

Banana Bread

1 jar Banana Bread Mix
1/2 C. butter or margarine,
   softened

2 eggs, slightly beaten
1 1/4 C. milk
1 tsp. vanilla

Preheat the oven to 350°F. In a large bowl, place the Banana Bread Mix. Make a well in the center. Mix wet ingredients and pour into dry mixture. Stir until the mixture is blended. Spoon the batter into a large loaf pan that is well greased with waxed paper in the bottom. Bake for 1 hour or until knife inserted in the center comes out clean. Cool in the pan on a wire rack before removing.

Banana Bread

1 jar Banana Bread Mix
1/2 C. butter or margarine,
   softened

2 eggs, slightly beaten
1 1/4 C. milk
1 tsp. vanilla

Preheat the oven to 350°F. In a large bowl, place the Banana Bread Mix. Make a well in the center. Mix wet ingredients and pour into dry mixture. Stir until the mixture is blended. Spoon the batter into a large loaf pan that is well greased with waxed paper in the bottom. Bake for 1 hour or until knife inserted in the center comes out clean. Cool in the pan on a wire rack before removing.

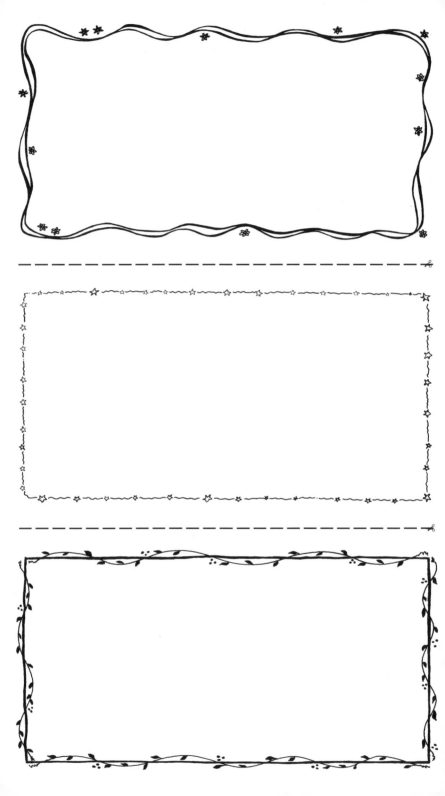

Banana Bread

1 jar Banana Bread Mix
1/2 C. butter or margarine,
  softened

2 eggs, slightly beaten
1 1/4 C. milk
1 tsp. vanilla

    Preheat the oven to 350°F. In a large bowl, place the Banana Bread Mix. Make a well in the center. Mix wet ingredients and pour into dry mixture. Stir until the mixture is blended. Spoon the batter into a large loaf pan that is well greased with waxed paper in the bottom. Bake for 1 hour or until knife inserted in the center comes out clean. Cool in the pan on a wire rack before removing.

Banana Bread

1 jar Banana Bread Mix
1/2 C. butter or margarine,
  softened

2 eggs, slightly beaten
1 1/4 C. milk
1 tsp. vanilla

    Preheat the oven to 350°F. In a large bowl, place the Banana Bread Mix. Make a well in the center. Mix wet ingredients and pour into dry mixture. Stir until the mixture is blended. Spoon the batter into a large loaf pan that is well greased with waxed paper in the bottom. Bake for 1 hour or until knife inserted in the center comes out clean. Cool in the pan on a wire rack before removing.

Banana Bread

1 jar Banana Bread Mix
1/2 C. butter or margarine,
  softened

2 eggs, slightly beaten
1 1/4 C. milk
1 tsp. vanilla

    Preheat the oven to 350°F. In a large bowl, place the Banana Bread Mix. Make a well in the center. Mix wet ingredients and pour into dry mixture. Stir until the mixture is blended. Spoon the batter into a large loaf pan that is well greased with waxed paper in the bottom. Bake for 1 hour or until knife inserted in the center comes out clean. Cool in the pan on a wire rack before removing.

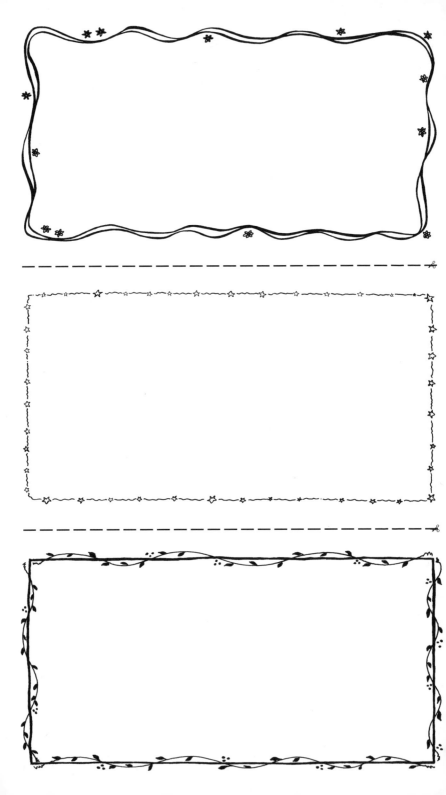

Heirloom Brown Bread Mix

2 C. whole wheat flour
1/2 C. all-purpose flour
2 tsp. baking soda
1 C. chopped dates
1 tsp. salt
1 C. raisins

Layer the ingredients in the order given into a wide-mouth 1-quart canning jar. Pack each layer in place before adding the next ingredient.

Attach a gift tag with the mixing and baking directions.

Heirloom Brown Bread

1 jar Heirloom Brown
   Bread Mix
2 C. buttermilk
1/2 C. molasses

Preheat the oven to 350°F. In a large bowl, place the Heirloom Brown Bread Mix. Make a well in the center. Mix wet ingredients and pour into dry mixture. Stir until the mixture is blended. Let stand at room temperature for 1/2 hour. Pour into a large loaf pan. Bake for 55 to 60 minutes. Cool in the pan on a wire rack before removing.

Heirloom Brown Bread

1 jar Heirloom Brown Bread Mix   1/2 C. molasses
2 C. buttermilk

Preheat the oven to 350°F. In a large bowl, place the Heirloom Brown Bread Mix. Make a well in the center. Mix wet ingredients and pour into dry mixture. Stir until the mixture is blended. Let stand at room temperature for 1/2 hour. Pour into a large loaf pan. Bake for 55 to 60 minutes. Cool in the pan on a wire rack before removing.

Heirloom Brown Bread

1 jar Heirloom Brown Bread Mix   1/2 C. molasses
2 C. buttermilk

Preheat the oven to 350°F. In a large bowl, place the Heirloom Brown Bread Mix. Make a well in the center. Mix wet ingredients and pour into dry mixture. Stir until the mixture is blended. Let stand at room temperature for 1/2 hour. Pour into a large loaf pan. Bake for 55 to 60 minutes. Cool in the pan on a wire rack before removing.

Heirloom Brown Bread

1 jar Heirloom Brown Bread Mix   1/2 C. molasses
2 C. buttermilk

Preheat the oven to 350°F. In a large bowl, place the Heirloom Brown Bread Mix. Make a well in the center. Mix wet ingredients and pour into dry mixture. Stir until the mixture is blended. Let stand at room temperature for 1/2 hour. Pour into a large loaf pan. Bake for 55 to 60 minutes. Cool in the pan on a wire rack before removing.

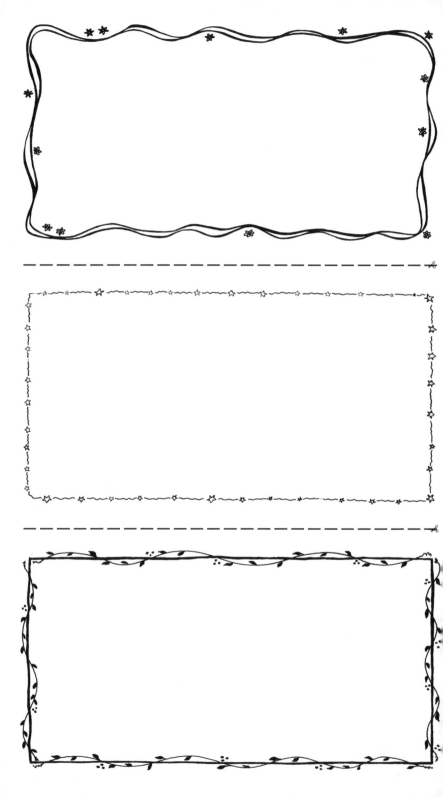

Heirloom Brown Bread

1 jar Heirloom Brown Bread Mix   1/2 C. molasses
2 C. buttermilk

Preheat the oven to 350°F. In a large bowl, place the Heirloom Brown Bread Mix. Make a well in the center. Mix wet ingredients and pour into dry mixture. Stir until the mixture is blended. Let stand at room temperature for 1/2 hour. Pour into a large loaf pan. Bake for 55 to 60 minutes. Cool in the pan on a wire rack before removing.

Heirloom Brown Bread

1 jar Heirloom Brown Bread Mix   1/2 C. molasses
2 C. buttermilk

Preheat the oven to 350°F. In a large bowl, place the Heirloom Brown Bread Mix. Make a well in the center. Mix wet ingredients and pour into dry mixture. Stir until the mixture is blended. Let stand at room temperature for 1/2 hour. Pour into a large loaf pan. Bake for 55 to 60 minutes. Cool in the pan on a wire rack before removing.

Heirloom Brown Bread

1 jar Heirloom Brown Bread Mix   1/2 C. molasses
2 C. buttermilk

Preheat the oven to 350°F. In a large bowl, place the Heirloom Brown Bread Mix. Make a well in the center. Mix wet ingredients and pour into dry mixture. Stir until the mixture is blended. Let stand at room temperature for 1/2 hour. Pour into a large loaf pan. Bake for 55 to 60 minutes. Cool in the pan on a wire rack before removing.

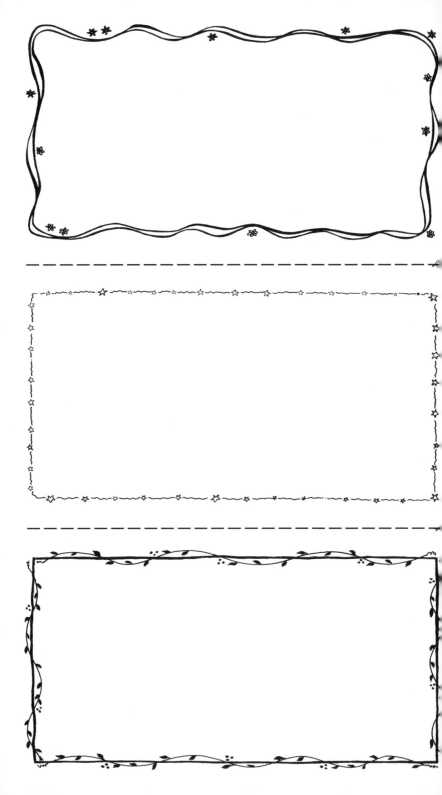

Blueberry Bread Mix

1/2 C. nuts
1/2 C. dried blueberries
1/2 C. sugar
2 1/2 C. Bisquick
1 tsp. baking powder
1/4 tsp. salt

Layer the ingredients in the order given into a wide-mouth 1-quart canning jar. Pack each layer in place before adding the next ingredient.

Attach a gift tag with the mixing and baking directions.

❀ *To make a gift in a jar fancier, decorate it with a doily and ribbon.* ❀

Blueberry Bread

1 jar Blueberry Bread Mix
1/2 C. butter or margarine,
 softened
2 eggs, slightly beaten
1 1/4 C. milk
1 tsp. vanilla

Preheat the oven to 350°F. In a large bowl, place the Blueberry Bread Mix. Make a well in the center. Mix wet ingredients and pour into dry mixture. Stir until the mixture is blended. Spoon the batter into a large loaf pan that is well greased with waxed paper in the bottom. Bake for 1 hour or until knife inserted in the center comes out clean. Cool in the pan on a wire rack before removing.

Blueberry Bread

1 jar Blueberry Bread Mix
1/2 C. butter or margarine,
 softened

2 eggs, slightly beaten
1 1/4 C. milk
1 tsp. vanilla

Preheat the oven to 350°F. In a large bowl, place the Blueberry Bread Mix. Make a well in the center. Mix wet ingredients and pour into dry mixture. Stir until the mixture is blended. Spoon the batter into a large loaf pan that is well greased with waxed paper in the bottom. Bake for 1 hour or until knife inserted in the center comes out clean. Cool in the pan on a wire rack before removing.

Blueberry Bread

1 jar Blueberry Bread Mix
1/2 C. butter or margarine,
 softened

2 eggs, slightly beaten
1 1/4 C. milk
1 tsp. vanilla

Preheat the oven to 350°F. In a large bowl, place the Blueberry Bread Mix. Make a well in the center. Mix wet ingredients and pour into dry mixture. Stir until the mixture is blended. Spoon the batter into a large loaf pan that is well greased with waxed paper in the bottom. Bake for 1 hour or until knife inserted in the center comes out clean. Cool in the pan on a wire rack before removing.

Blueberry Bread

1 jar Blueberry Bread Mix
1/2 C. butter or margarine,
 softened

2 eggs, slightly beaten
1 1/4 C. milk
1 tsp. vanilla

Preheat the oven to 350°F. In a large bowl, place the Blueberry Bread Mix. Make a well in the center. Mix wet ingredients and pour into dry mixture. Stir until the mixture is blended. Spoon the batter into a large loaf pan that is well greased with waxed paper in the bottom. Bake for 1 hour or until knife inserted in the center comes out clean. Cool in the pan on a wire rack before removing.

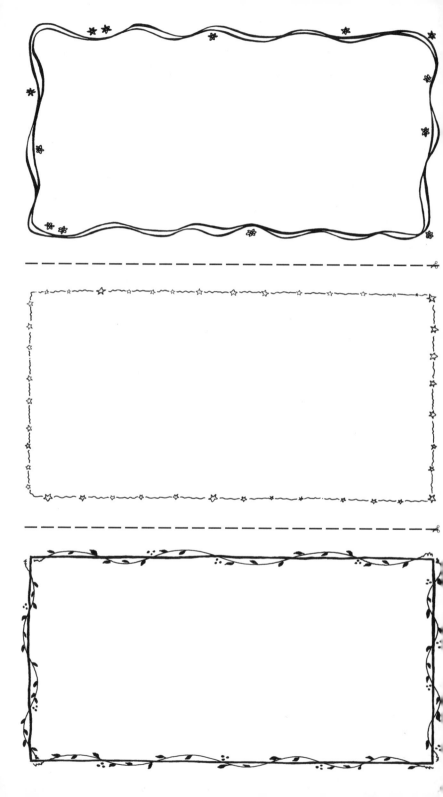

Blueberry Bread

1 jar Blueberry Bread Mix
1/2 C. butter or margarine,
  softened

2 eggs, slightly beaten
1 1/4 C. milk
1 tsp. vanilla

    Preheat the oven to 350°F. In a large bowl, place the Blueberry Bread Mix. Make a well in the center. Mix wet ingredients and pour into dry mixture. Stir until the mixture is blended. Spoon the batter into a large loaf pan that is well greased with waxed paper in the bottom. Bake for 1 hour or until knife inserted in the center comes out clean. Cool in the pan on a wire rack before removing.

Blueberry Bread

1 jar Blueberry Bread Mix
1/2 C. butter or margarine,
  softened

2 eggs, slightly beaten
1 1/4 C. milk
1 tsp. vanilla

    Preheat the oven to 350°F. In a large bowl, place the Blueberry Bread Mix. Make a well in the center. Mix wet ingredients and pour into dry mixture. Stir until the mixture is blended. Spoon the batter into a large loaf pan that is well greased with waxed paper in the bottom. Bake for 1 hour or until knife inserted in the center comes out clean. Cool in the pan on a wire rack before removing.

Blueberry Bread

1 jar Blueberry Bread Mix
1/2 C. butter or margarine,
  softened

2 eggs, slightly beaten
1 1/4 C. milk
1 tsp. vanilla

    Preheat the oven to 350°F. In a large bowl, place the Blueberry Bread Mix. Make a well in the center. Mix wet ingredients and pour into dry mixture. Stir until the mixture is blended. Spoon the batter into a large loaf pan that is well greased with waxed paper in the bottom. Bake for 1 hour or until knife inserted in the center comes out clean. Cool in the pan on a wire rack before removing.

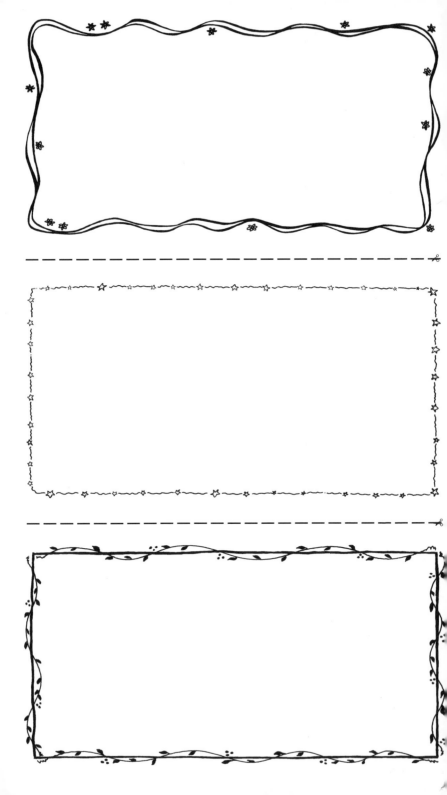

Banana Chocolate Chip Bread Mix

1/2 C. chocolate chips
1/2 C. finely chopped dried
   bananas
1/2 C. sugar
2 1/2 C. Bisquick
1 tsp. baking powder
1/4 tsp. salt

Layer the ingredients in the order given into a wide-mouth 1-quart canning jar. Pack each layer in place before adding the next ingredient.

Attach a gift tag with the mixing and baking directions.

Banana Chocolate Chip Bread

1 jar Banana Chocolate Chip
  Bread Mix
1/2 C. butter or margarine,
  softened
2 eggs, slightly beaten
1 1/4 C. milk
1 tsp. vanilla

Preheat the oven to 350°F. In a large bowl, place the Banana Chocolate Chip Bread Mix. Make a well in the center. Mix wet ingredients and pour into dry mixture. Stir until the mixture is blended. Spoon the batter into a large loaf pan that is well greased with waxed paper in the bottom. Bake for 1 hour or until knife inserted in the center comes out clean. Cool in the pan on a wire rack before removing.

Banana Chocolate Chip Bread

1 jar Banana Chocolate
  Chip Bread Mix
1/2 C. butter or margarine,
  softened

2 eggs, slightly beaten
1 1/4 C. milk
1 tsp. vanilla

Preheat the oven to 350°F. In a large bowl, place the Banana Chocolate Chip Bread Mix. Make a well in the center. Mix wet ingredients and pour into dry mixture. Stir until the mixture is blended. Spoon the batter into a large loaf pan that is well greased with waxed paper in the bottom. Bake for 1 hour or until knife inserted in the center comes out clean. Cool in the pan on a wire rack before removing.

Banana Chocolate Chip Bread

1 jar Banana Chocolate
  Chip Bread Mix
1/2 C. butter or margarine,
  softened

2 eggs, slightly beaten
1 1/4 C. milk
1 tsp. vanilla

Preheat the oven to 350°F. In a large bowl, place the Banana Chocolate Chip Bread Mix. Make a well in the center. Mix wet ingredients and pour into dry mixture. Stir until the mixture is blended. Spoon the batter into a large loaf pan that is well greased with waxed paper in the bottom. Bake for 1 hour or until knife inserted in the center comes out clean. Cool in the pan on a wire rack before removing.

Banana Chocolate Chip Bread

1 jar Banana Chocolate
  Chip Bread Mix
1/2 C. butter or margarine,
  softened

2 eggs, slightly beaten
1 1/4 C. milk
1 tsp. vanilla

Preheat the oven to 350°F. In a large bowl, place the Banana Chocolate Chip Bread Mix. Make a well in the center. Mix wet ingredients and pour into dry mixture. Stir until the mixture is blended. Spoon the batter into a large loaf pan that is well greased with waxed paper in the bottom. Bake for 1 hour or until knife inserted in the center comes out clean. Cool in the pan on a wire rack before removing.

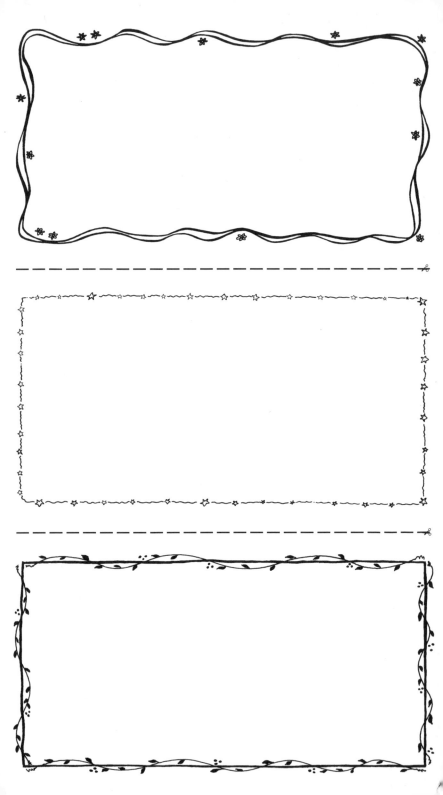

Banana Chocolate Chip Bread

1 jar Banana Chocolate
  Chip Bread Mix
1/2 C. butter or margarine,
  softened

2 eggs, slightly beaten
1 1/4 C. milk
1 tsp. vanilla

Preheat the oven to 350°F. In a large bowl, place the Banana Chocolate Chip Bread Mix. Make a well in the center. Mix wet ingredients and pour into dry mixture. Stir until the mixture is blended. Spoon the batter into a large loaf pan that is well greased with waxed paper in the bottom. Bake for 1 hour or until knife inserted in the center comes out clean. Cool in the pan on a wire rack before removing.

Banana Chocolate Chip Bread

1 jar Banana Chocolate
  Chip Bread Mix
1/2 C. butter or margarine,
  softened

2 eggs, slightly beaten
1 1/4 C. milk
1 tsp. vanilla

Preheat the oven to 350°F. In a large bowl, place the Banana Chocolate Chip Bread Mix. Make a well in the center. Mix wet ingredients and pour into dry mixture. Stir until the mixture is blended. Spoon the batter into a large loaf pan that is well greased with waxed paper in the bottom. Bake for 1 hour or until knife inserted in the center comes out clean. Cool in the pan on a wire rack before removing.

Banana Chocolate Chip Bread

1 jar Banana Chocolate
  Chip Bread Mix
1/2 C. butter or margarine,
  softened

2 eggs, slightly beaten
1 1/4 C. milk
1 tsp. vanilla

Preheat the oven to 350°F. In a large bowl, place the Banana Chocolate Chip Bread Mix. Make a well in the center. Mix wet ingredients and pour into dry mixture. Stir until the mixture is blended. Spoon the batter into a large loaf pan that is well greased with waxed paper in the bottom. Bake for 1 hour or until knife inserted in the center comes out clean. Cool in the pan on a wire rack before removing.

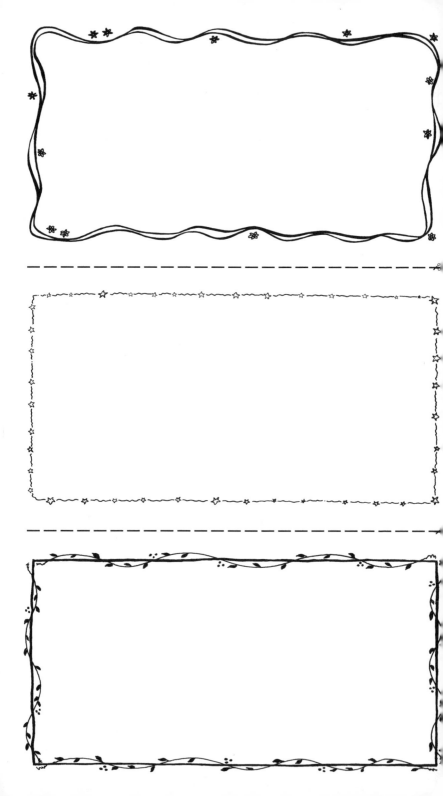

Whole Wheat Beer Bread Mix

2 1/2 C. self-rising flour
1/2 C. whole wheat flour
3 T. sugar

Layer the ingredients in the order given into a wide-mouth 1-quart canning jar. Pack each layer in place before adding the next ingredient.

Attach a gift tag with the mixing and baking directions.

Whole Wheat Beer Bread

1 jar Whole Wheat Beer
   Bread Mix
1 (12 ounce) bottle of beer,
   or 1 (12 ounce) bottle
   unflavored seltzer
1/2 C. butter or margarine,
   melted

Preheat the oven to 375°F. In a large bowl, combine the Whole Wheat Beer Bread Mix with the beer or seltzer. Blend the mixture together, using a wooden spoon. The batter will be lumpy. Place the dough in a greased loaf pan. Pour 1/3 of the butter over the dough. Bake the bread for 40 minutes, then pour 1/3 of the butter over the top of the bread. Continue baking for 10 minutes more. Pour the last 1/3 of the butter on the bread and bake 10 minutes longer. Remove the bread from the oven. Allow the bread to cool for 30 to 45 minutes and serve warm.

Whole Wheat Beer Bread

1 jar Whole Wheat Beer Bread Mix
1 (12 ounce) bottle of beer, or 1
  (12 ounce) bottle unflavored
  seltzer

1/2 C. butter or margarine,
  melted

Preheat the oven to 375°F. In a large bowl, combine the Whole Wheat Beer Bread Mix with the beer or seltzer. Blend the mixture together, using a wooden spoon. The batter will be lumpy. Place the dough in a greased loaf pan. Pour 1/3 of the butter over the dough. Bake the bread for 40 minutes, then pour 1/3 of the butter over the top of the bread. Continue baking for 10 minutes more. Pour the last 1/3 of the butter on the bread and bake 10 minutes longer. Remove the bread from the oven. Allow the bread to cool for 30 to 45 minutes and serve warm.

Whole Wheat Beer Bread

1 jar Whole Wheat Beer Bread Mix
1 (12 ounce) bottle of beer, or 1
  (12 ounce) bottle unflavored
  seltzer

1/2 C. butter or margarine,
  melted

Preheat the oven to 375°F. In a large bowl, combine the Whole Wheat Beer Bread Mix with the beer or seltzer. Blend the mixture together, using a wooden spoon. The batter will be lumpy. Place the dough in a greased loaf pan. Pour 1/3 of the butter over the dough. Bake the bread for 40 minutes, then pour 1/3 of the butter over the top of the bread. Continue baking for 10 minutes more. Pour the last 1/3 of the butter on the bread and bake 10 minutes longer. Remove the bread from the oven. Allow the bread to cool for 30 to 45 minutes and serve warm.

Whole Wheat Beer Bread

1 jar Whole Wheat Beer Bread Mix
1 (12 ounce) bottle of beer, or 1
  (12 ounce) bottle unflavored
  seltzer

1/2 C. butter or margarine,
  melted

Preheat the oven to 375°F. In a large bowl, combine the Whole Wheat Beer Bread Mix with the beer or seltzer. Blend the mixture together, using a wooden spoon. The batter will be lumpy. Place the dough in a greased loaf pan. Pour 1/3 of the butter over the dough. Bake the bread for 40 minutes, then pour 1/3 of the butter over the top of the bread. Continue baking for 10 minutes more. Pour the last 1/3 of the butter on the bread and bake 10 minutes longer. Remove the bread from the oven. Allow the bread to cool for 30 to 45 minutes and serve warm.

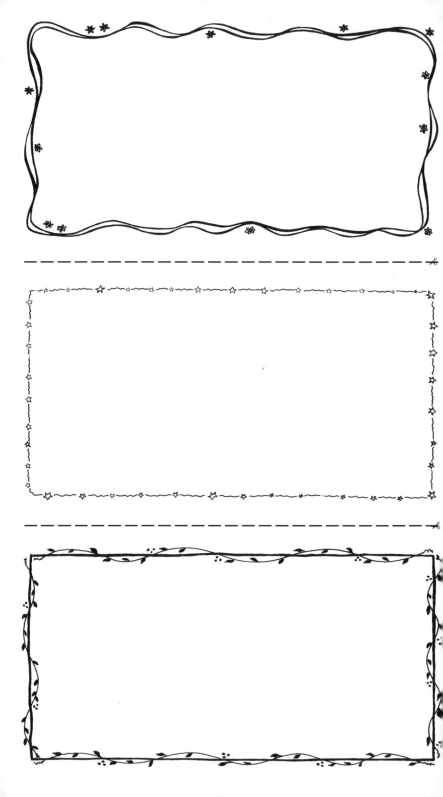

Whole Wheat Beer Bread

1 jar Whole Wheat Beer Bread Mix
1 (12 ounce) bottle of beer, or 1
    (12 ounce) bottle unflavored
    seltzer

1/2 C. butter or margarine,
    melted

Preheat the oven to 375°F. In a large bowl, combine the Whole Wheat Beer Bread Mix with the beer or seltzer. Blend the mixture together, using a wooden spoon. The batter will be lumpy. Place the dough in a greased loaf pan. Pour 1/3 of the butter over the dough. Bake the bread for 40 minutes, then pour 1/3 of the butter over the top of the bread. Continue baking for 10 minutes more. Pour the last 1/3 of the butter on the bread and bake 10 minutes longer. Remove the bread from the oven. Allow the bread to cool for 30 to 45 minutes and serve warm.

Whole Wheat Beer Bread

1 jar Whole Wheat Beer Bread Mix
1 (12 ounce) bottle of beer, or 1
    (12 ounce) bottle unflavored
    seltzer

1/2 C. butter or margarine,
    melted

Preheat the oven to 375°F. In a large bowl, combine the Whole Wheat Beer Bread Mix with the beer or seltzer. Blend the mixture together, using a wooden spoon. The batter will be lumpy. Place the dough in a greased loaf pan. Pour 1/3 of the butter over the dough. Bake the bread for 40 minutes, then pour 1/3 of the butter over the top of the bread. Continue baking for 10 minutes more. Pour the last 1/3 of the butter on the bread and bake 10 minutes longer. Remove the bread from the oven. Allow the bread to cool for 30 to 45 minutes and serve warm.

Whole Wheat Beer Bread

1 jar Whole Wheat Beer Bread Mix
1 (12 ounce) bottle of beer, or 1
    (12 ounce) bottle unflavored
    seltzer

1/2 C. butter or margarine,
    melted

Preheat the oven to 375°F. In a large bowl, combine the Whole Wheat Beer Bread Mix with the beer or seltzer. Blend the mixture together, using a wooden spoon. The batter will be lumpy. Place the dough in a greased loaf pan. Pour 1/3 of the butter over the dough. Bake the bread for 40 minutes, then pour 1/3 of the butter over the top of the bread. Continue baking for 10 minutes more. Pour the last 1/3 of the butter on the bread and bake 10 minutes longer. Remove the bread from the oven. Allow the bread to cool for 30 to 45 minutes and serve warm.

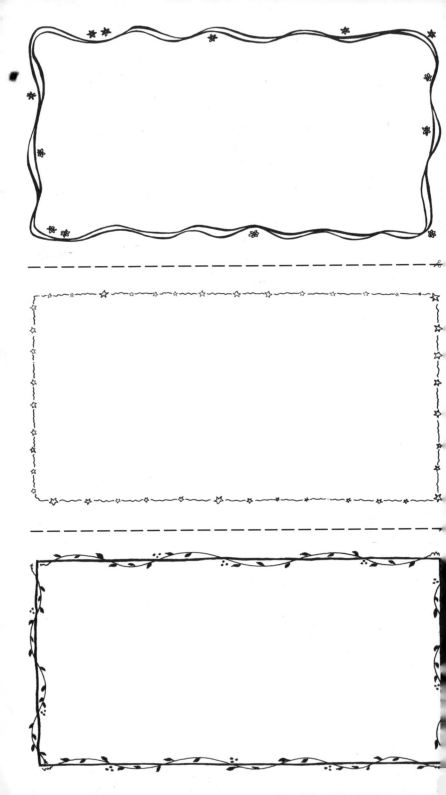